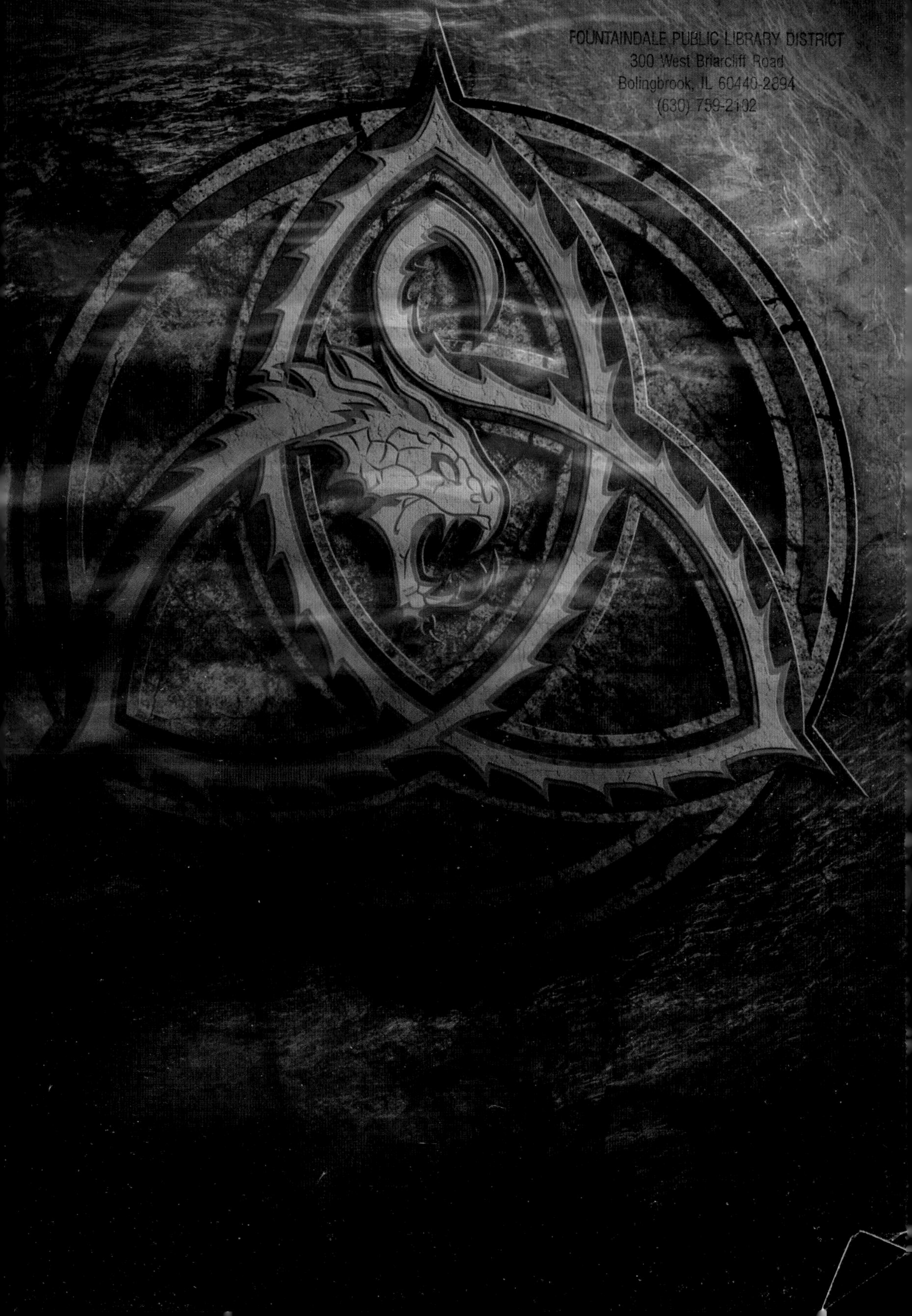

FEAR
ITSELF
SPIDER-MAN

WRITER
CHRIS YOST

ARTIST
MIKE McKONE

COLORS
JEROMY COX

LETTERS
VC'S JOE CARAMAGNA

COVER ART
MARKO DJURDJEVIC

ASSISTANT EDITOR
ELLIE PYLE

EDITOR
STEPHEN WACKER

FEAR ITSELF: FF
WRITER: **CULLEN BUNN**
PENCILER: **TOM GRUMMETT**
INKERS: **CORY HAMSCHER**
WITH RICK MAGYAR
COLORIST: **RAIN BEREDO**
LETTERER: **VC'S CLAYTON COWLES**
COVER ARTIST: **GABRIELE DELL'OTTO**
ASSOCIATE EDITOR: **LAUREN SANKOVITCH**
TOM BREV

FEAR ITSELF: THE WORTHY
WRITERS: **CHRISTOS GAGE, JEFF PARKER, JEN VAN METER, FRANK TIERI, GREG PAK, TOM DEFALCO, TOM PEYER & ROBERTO AGUIRRE-SACASA**

ARTISTS: **ELIA BONETTI, DECLAN SHALVEY, CLAYTON HENRY, ERIC CANETE, LEE WEEKS MARIO ALBERTI, SERGIO CARIELLO & JAVIER PULIDO**

COLORISTS: **MATTHEW WILSON, FRANK MARTIN JR. CHRIS CHUCKRY, MARIO ALBERTI**

PREVIOUSLY:

A time of uncertainty and fear grips the world.

Sin, the daughter of the Red Skull, has unleashed an ancient evil into the world: the forgotten Asgardian god known only as the Serpent! He has summoned forth seven mystical hammers from the cosmos, and those that grasp these hammers become uncontrollable engines of destruction. With his hammer-wielding minions, the Serpent devastates the Earth in his march towards revenge on Odin and Asgard.

COLLECTION EDITOR: JENNIFER GRÜNWALD • ASSISTANT EDITORS: ALEX STARBUCK & NELSON RIBEIRO
EDITOR, SPECIAL PROJECTS: MARK D. BEAZLEY • SENIOR EDITOR, SPECIAL PROJECTS: JEFF YOUNGQUIST
SENIOR VICE PRESIDENT OF SALES: DAVID GABRIEL • SVP OF BRAND PLANNING & COMMUNICATIONS: MICHAEL PASCIULLO

EDITOR IN CHIEF: AXEL ALONSO • CHIEF CREATIVE OFFICER: JOE QUESADA • PUBLISHER: DAN BUCKLEY • EXECUTIVE PRODUCER: ALAN FINE

EAR ITSELF: SPIDER-MAN. Contains material originally published in magazine form as FEAR ITSELF SPIDER-MAN #1-3, FEAR ITSELF: FF #1 and FEAR ITSELF: THE WORTHY #1. First printing 2012. ISBN# 978-0-7851-
703-8. Published by MARVEL WORLDWIDE, INC., a subsidiary of MARVEL ENTERTAINMENT, LLC. OFFICE OF PUBLICATION: 135 West 50th Street, New York, NY 10020. Copyright © 2011 and 2012 Marvel Characters,
c. All rights reserved. $16.99 per copy in the U.S. and $18.99 in Canada (GST #R127032852); Canadian Agreement #40668537. All characters featured in this issue and the distinctive names and likenesses thereof,
d all related indicia are trademarks of Marvel Characters, Inc. No similarity between any of the names, characters, persons, and/or institutions in this magazine with those of any living or dead person or institution is
tended, and any such similarity which may exist is purely coincidental. **Printed in the U.S.A.** ALAN FINE, EVP - Office of the President, Marvel Worldwide, Inc. and EVP & CMO Marvel Characters B.V.; DAN BUCKLEY,
blisher & President - Print, Animation & Digital Divisions; JOE QUESADA, Chief Creative Officer; TOM BREVOORT, SVP of Publishing; DAVID BOGART, SVP of Operations & Procurement, Publishing; RUWAN JAYATILLEKE,
P & Associate Publisher, Publishing; C.B. CEBULSKI, SVP of Creator & Content Development; DAVID GABRIEL, SVP of Publishing Sales & Circulation; MICHAEL PASCIULLO, SVP of Brand Planning & Communications;
M O'KEEFE, VP of Operations & Logistics; DAN CARR, Executive Director of Publishing Technology; SUSAN CRESPI, Editorial Operations Manager; ALEX MORALES, Publishing Operations Manager; STAN LEE, Chairman
meritus. For information regarding advertising in Marvel Comics or on Marvel.com, please contact Niza Disla, Director of Marvel Partnerships, at ndisla@marvel.com. For Marvel subscription inquiries, please call 800-
17-9158. **Manufactured between 8/29/2012 and 10/1/2012 by R.R. DONNELLEY, INC., SALEM, VA, USA.**

0987654321

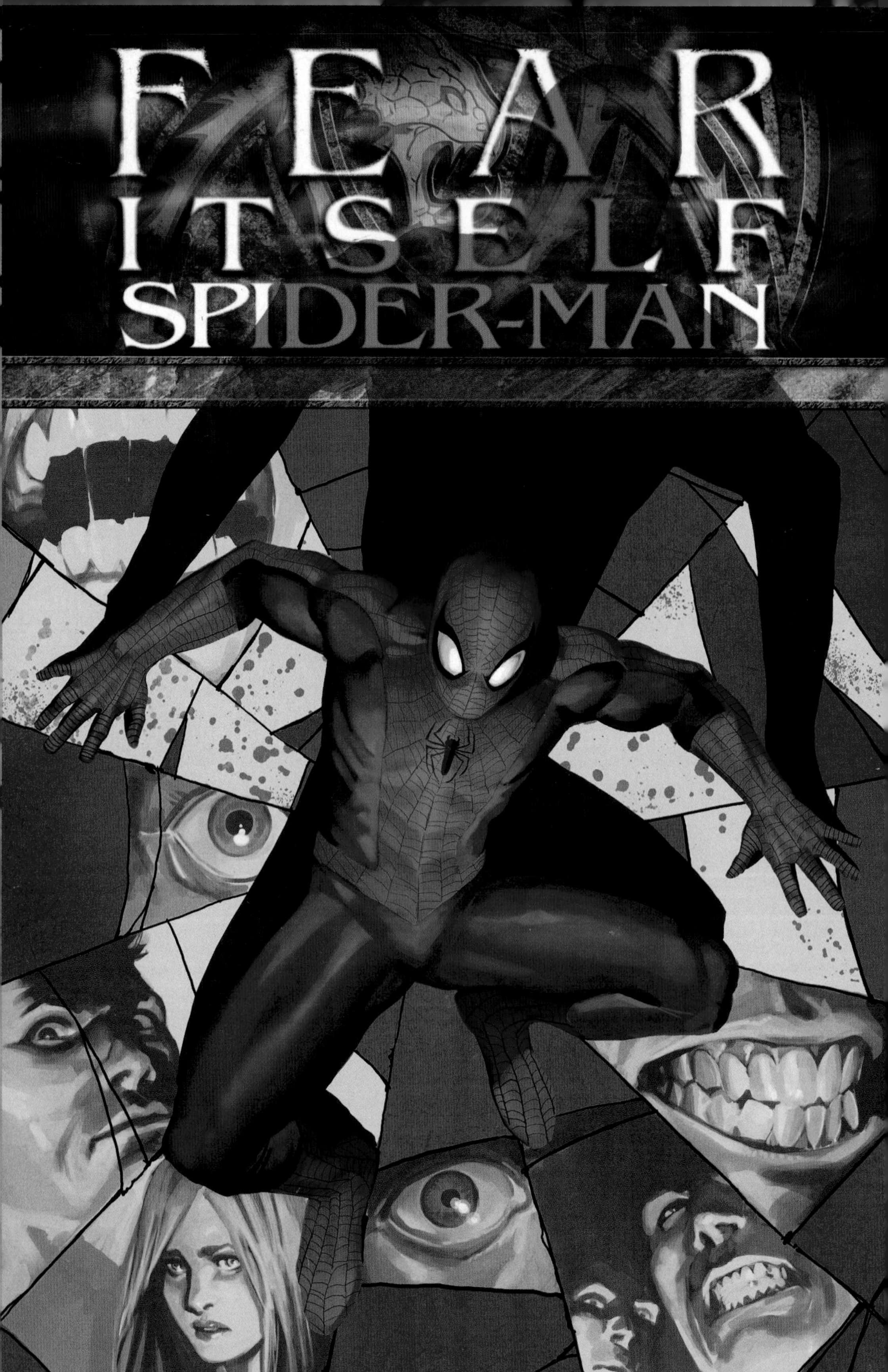
FEAR
ITSELF
SPIDER-MAN

New York City.
Hour Six Of The Fear.

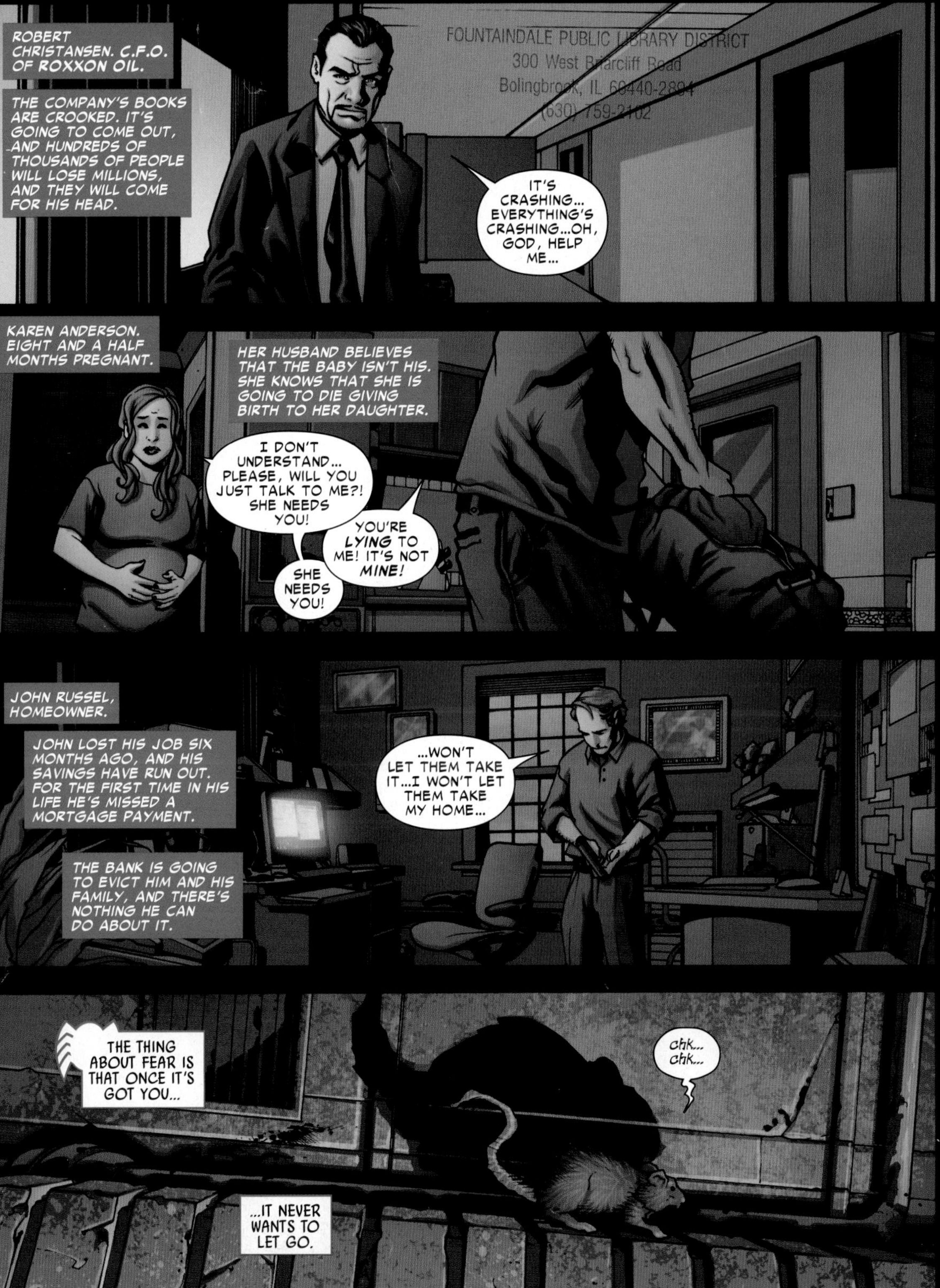

ROBERT CHRISTANSEN. C.F.O. OF ROXXON OIL.
THE COMPANY'S BOOKS ARE CROOKED. IT'S GOING TO COME OUT, AND HUNDREDS OF THOUSANDS OF PEOPLE WILL LOSE MILLIONS, AND THEY WILL COME FOR HIS HEAD.
IT'S CRASHING... EVERYTHING'S CRASHING...OH, GOD, HELP ME...
KAREN ANDERSON. EIGHT AND A HALF MONTHS PREGNANT.
HER HUSBAND BELIEVES THAT THE BABY ISN'T HIS. SHE KNOWS THAT SHE IS GOING TO DIE GIVING BIRTH TO HER DAUGHTER.
I DON'T UNDERSTAND... PLEASE, WILL YOU JUST TALK TO ME?! SHE NEEDS YOU!
YOU'RE LYING TO ME! IT'S NOT MINE!
SHE NEEDS YOU!
JOHN RUSSEL, HOMEOWNER.
JOHN LOST HIS JOB SIX MONTHS AGO, AND HIS SAVINGS HAVE RUN OUT. FOR THE FIRST TIME IN HIS LIFE HE'S MISSED A MORTGAGE PAYMENT.
THE BANK IS GOING TO EVICT HIM AND HIS FAMILY, AND THERE'S NOTHING HE CAN DO ABOUT IT.
...WON'T LET THEM TAKE IT...I WON'T LET THEM TAKE MY HOME...
THE THING ABOUT FEAR IS THAT ONCE IT'S GOT YOU...
chk... chk...
...IT NEVER WANTS TO LET GO.

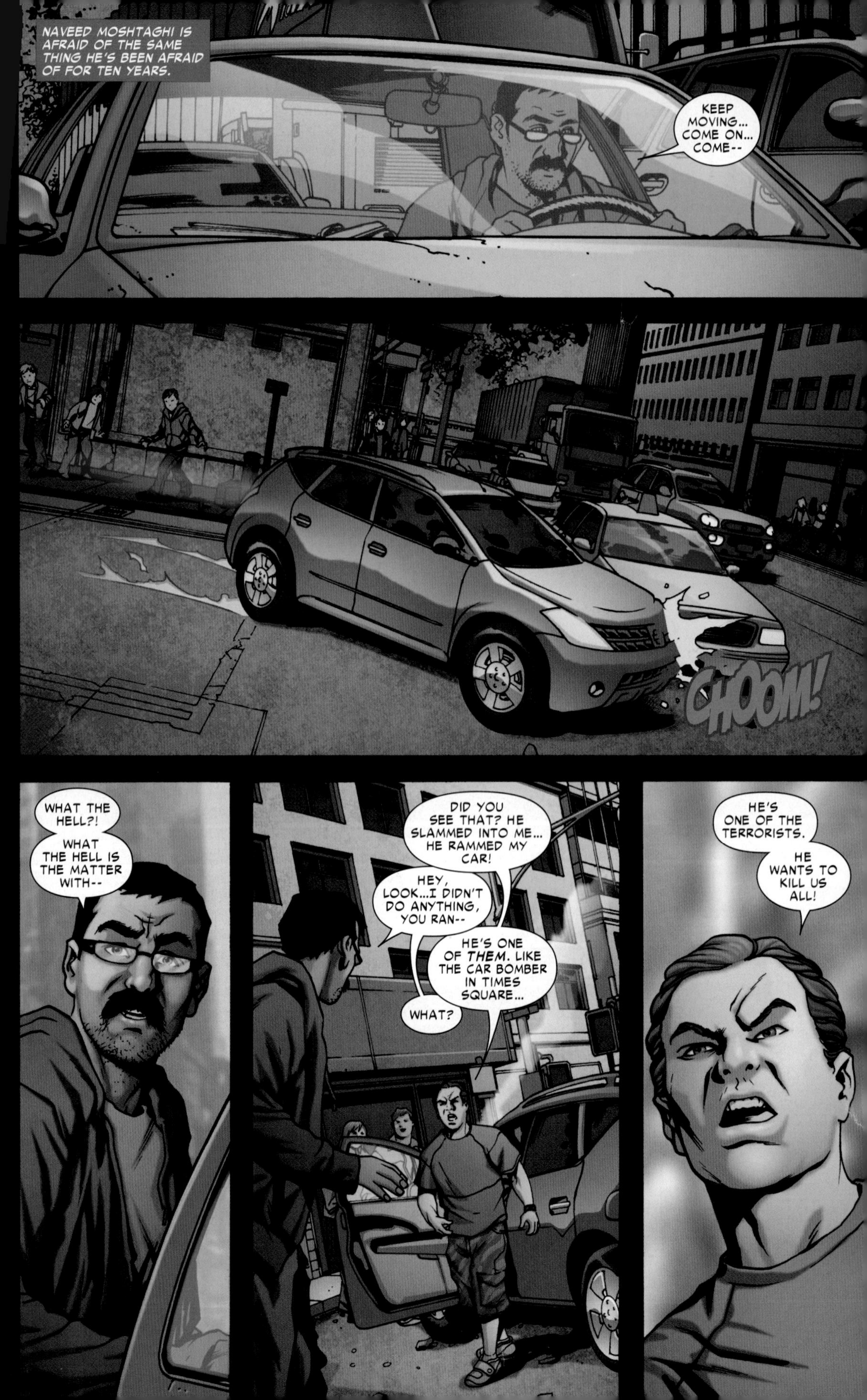
NAVEED MOSHTAGHI IS AFRAID OF THE SAME THING HE'S BEEN AFRAID OF FOR TEN YEARS.
KEEP MOVING... COME ON... COME--
CHOOM!
WHAT THE HELL?!
WHAT THE HELL IS THE MATTER WITH--
DID YOU SEE THAT? HE SLAMMED INTO ME... HE RAMMED MY CAR!
HEY, LOOK...I DIDN'T DO ANYTHING, YOU RAN--
HE'S ONE OF *THEM*. LIKE THE CAR BOMBER IN TIMES SQUARE...
WHAT?
HE'S ONE OF THE TERRORISTS.
HE WANTS TO KILL US ALL!

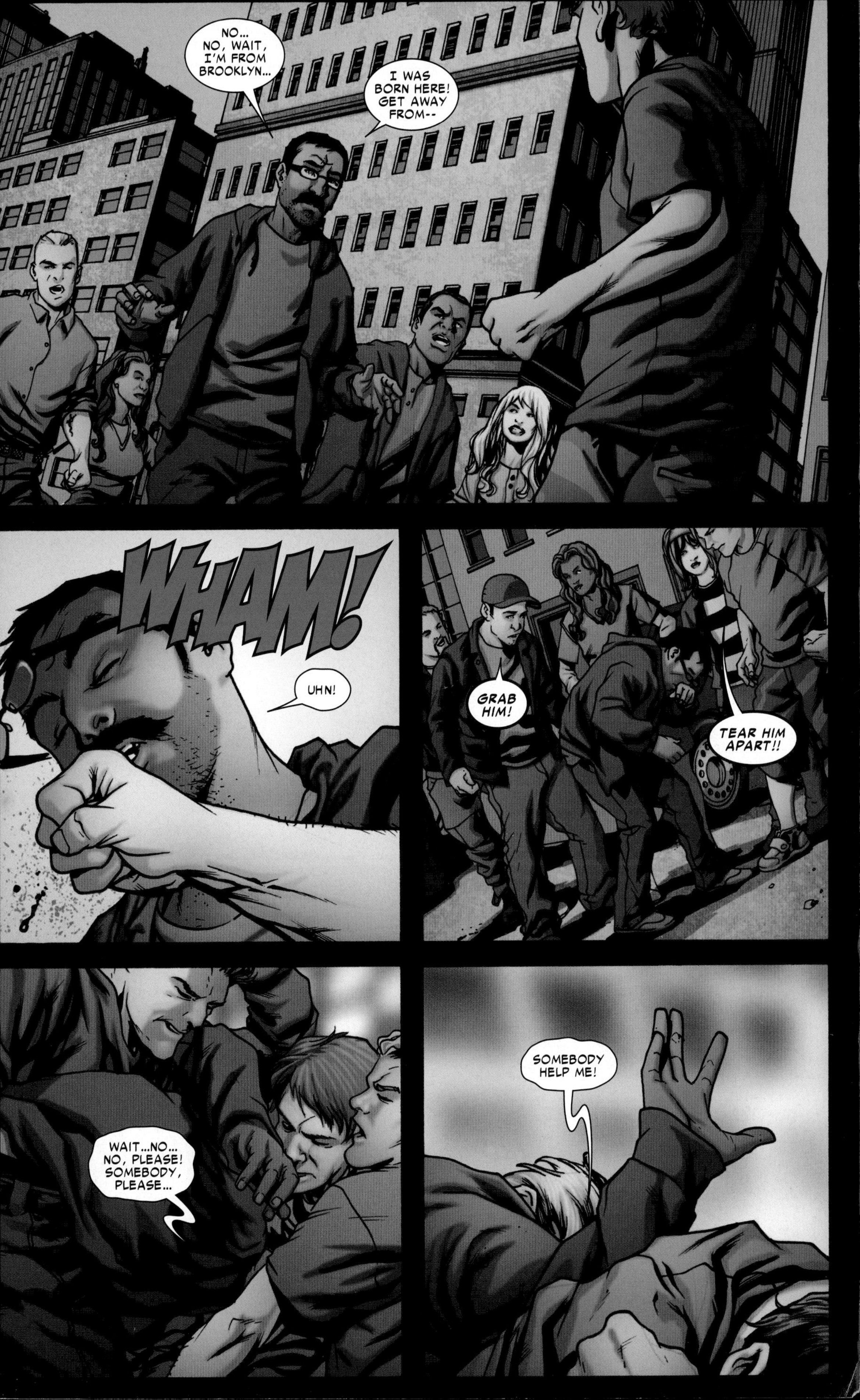
NO... NO, WAIT, I'M FROM BROOKLYN...
I WAS BORN HERE! GET AWAY FROM--
WHAM!
UHN!
GRAB HIM!
TEAR HIM APART!!
WAIT...NO... NO, PLEASE! SOMEBODY, PLEASE...
SOMEBODY HELP ME!

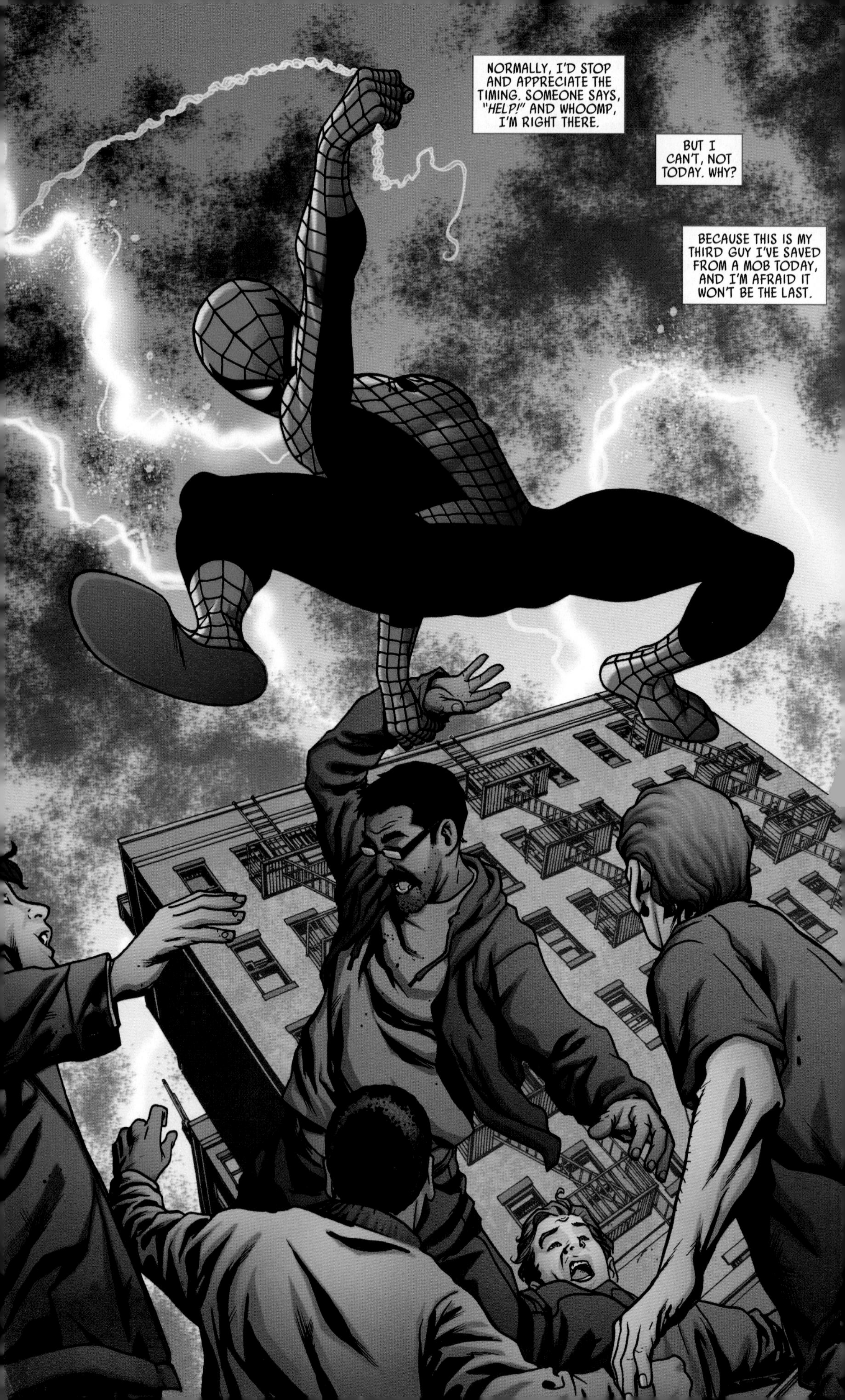
NORMALLY, I'D STOP AND APPRECIATE THE TIMING. SOMEONE SAYS, "*HELP!*" AND WHOOMP, I'M RIGHT THERE.
BUT I CAN'T, NOT TODAY. WHY?
BECAUSE THIS IS MY THIRD GUY I'VE SAVED FROM A MOB TODAY, AND I'M AFRAID IT WON'T BE THE LAST.

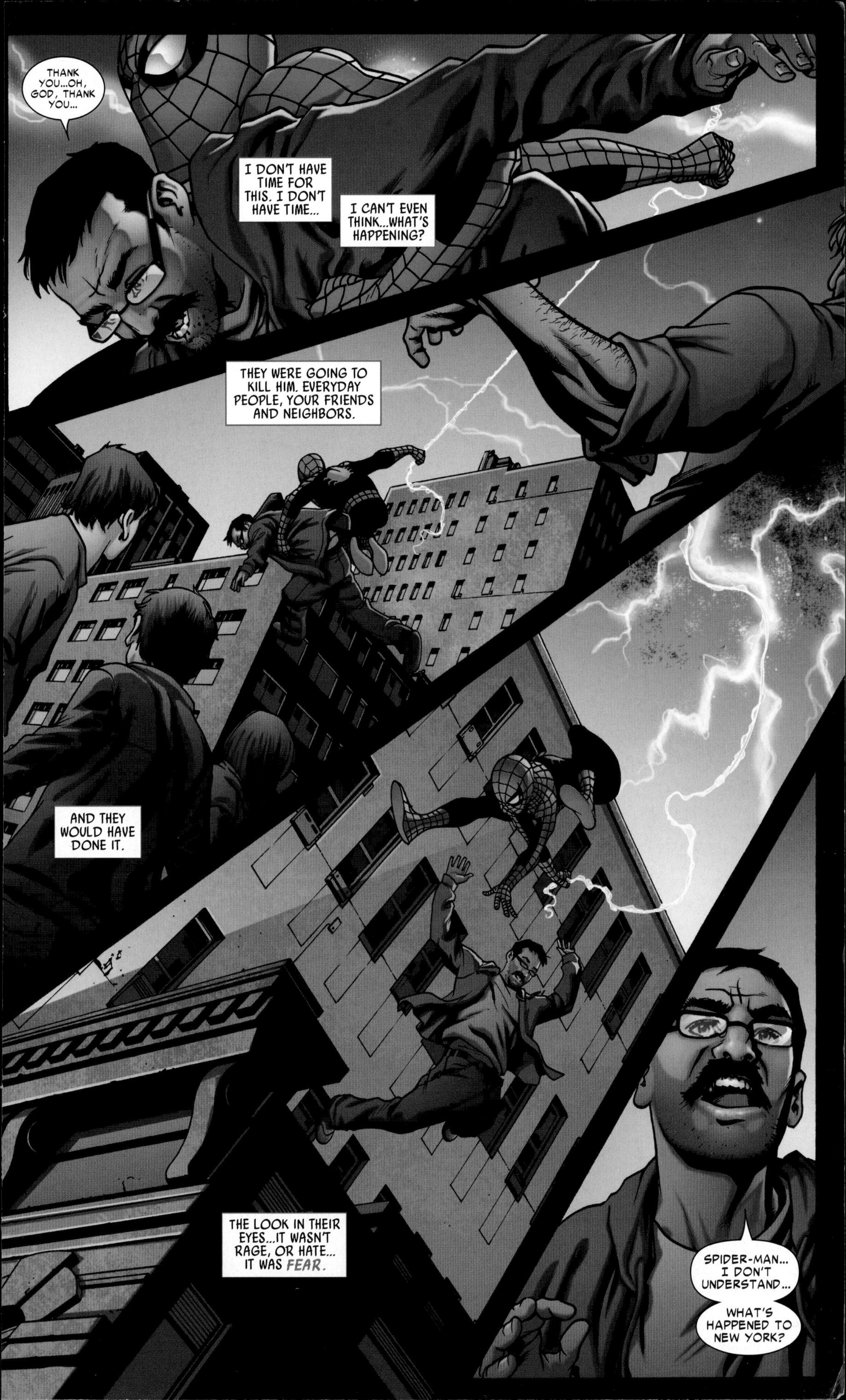
THANK YOU...OH, GOD, THANK YOU...
I DON'T HAVE TIME FOR THIS. I DON'T HAVE TIME...
I CAN'T EVEN THINK...WHAT'S HAPPENING?
THEY WERE GOING TO KILL HIM. EVERYDAY PEOPLE, YOUR FRIENDS AND NEIGHBORS.
AND THEY WOULD HAVE DONE IT.
THE LOOK IN THEIR EYES...IT WASN'T RAGE, OR HATE... IT WAS FEAR.
SPIDER-MAN... I DON'T UNDERSTAND...
WHAT'S HAPPENED TO NEW YORK?

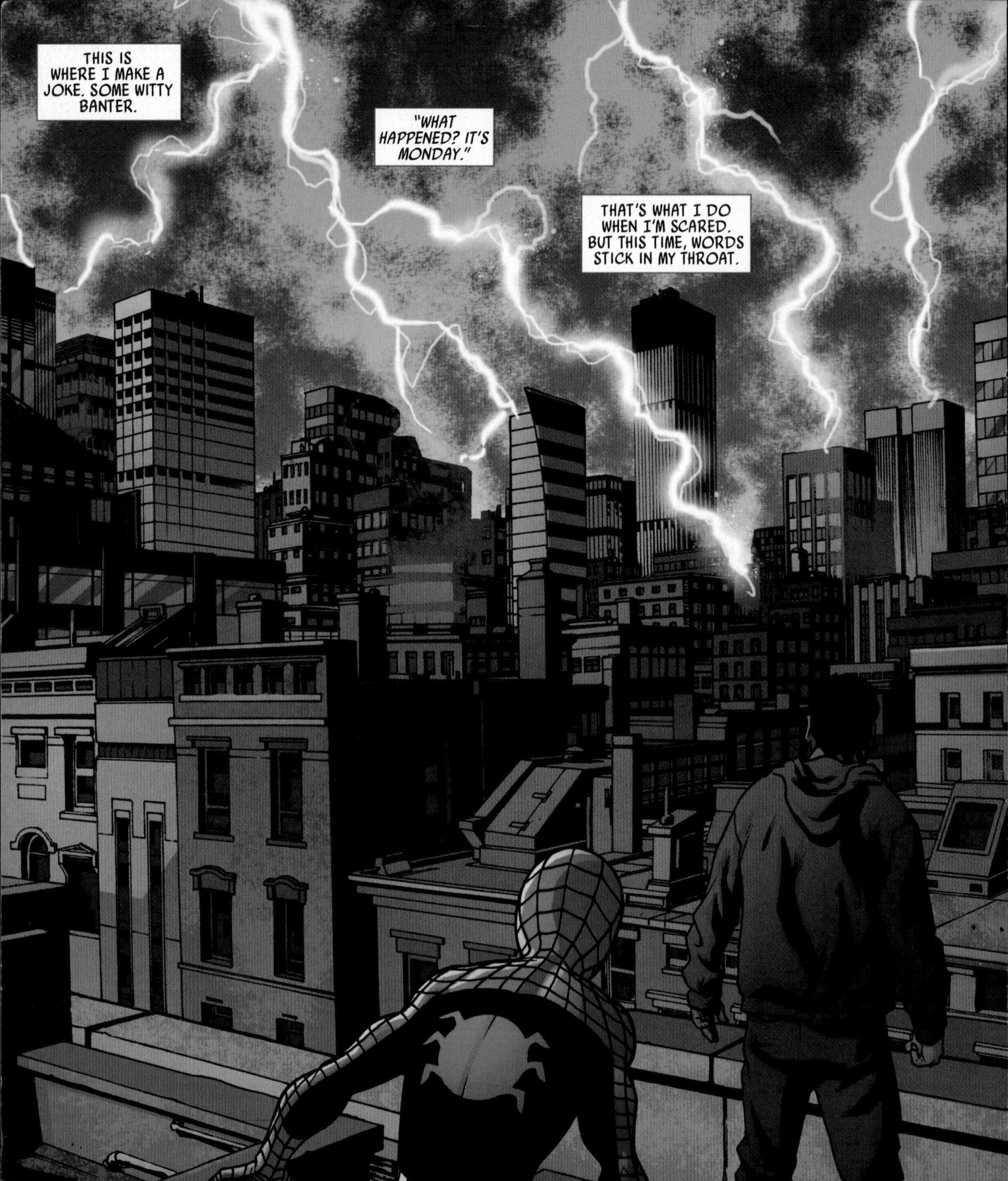
THIS IS WHERE I MAKE A JOKE. SOME WITTY BANTER.
"WHAT HAPPENED? IT'S MONDAY."
THAT'S WHAT I DO WHEN I'M SCARED. BUT THIS TIME, WORDS STICK IN MY THROAT.

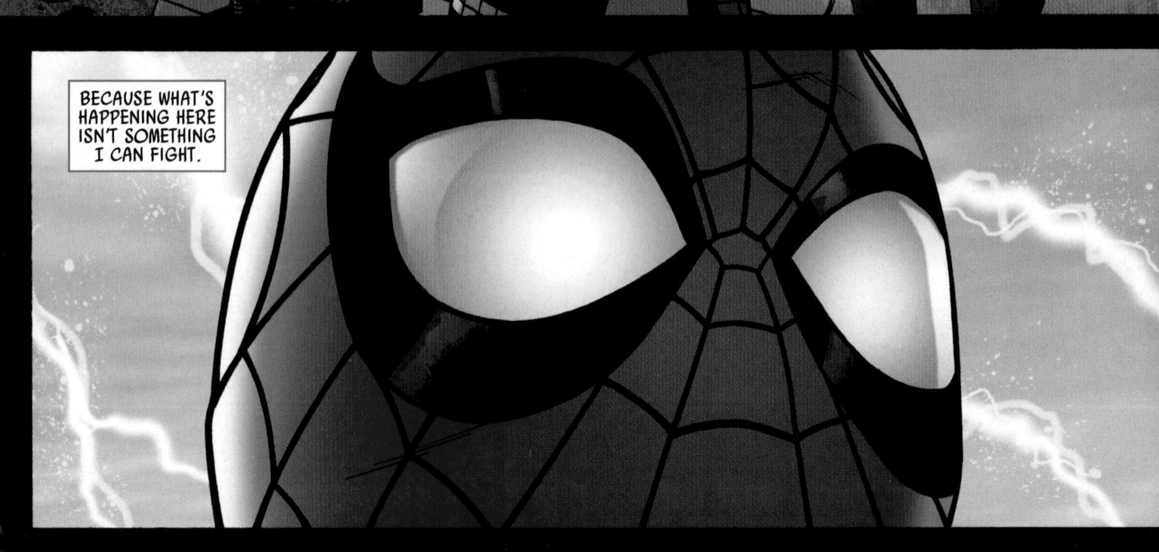
BECAUSE WHAT'S HAPPENING HERE ISN'T SOMETHING I CAN FIGHT.

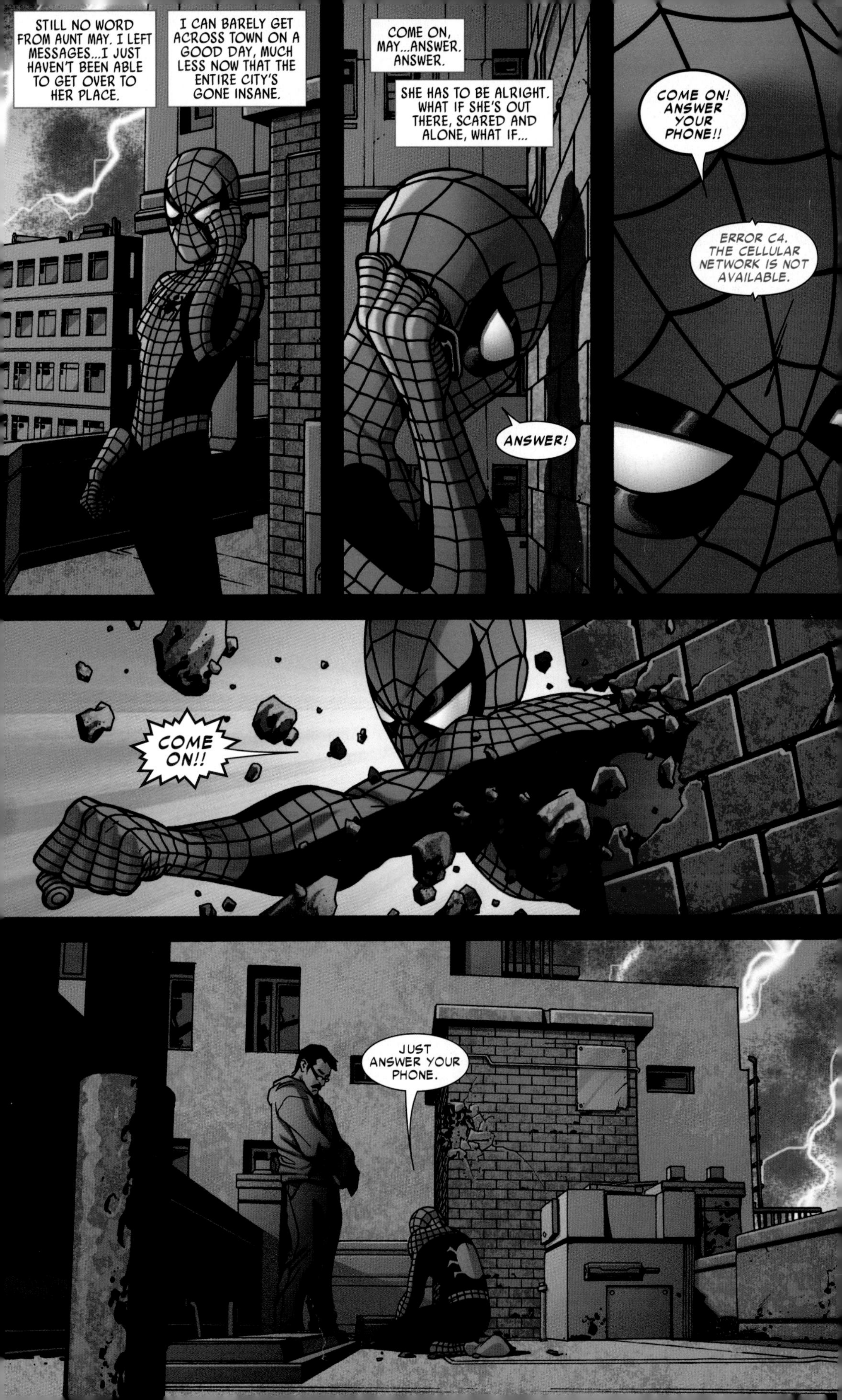
STILL NO WORD FROM AUNT MAY. I LEFT MESSAGES...I JUST HAVEN'T BEEN ABLE TO GET OVER TO HER PLACE.
I CAN BARELY GET ACROSS TOWN ON A GOOD DAY, MUCH LESS NOW THAT THE ENTIRE CITY'S GONE INSANE.
COME ON, MAY...ANSWER. ANSWER.
SHE HAS TO BE ALRIGHT. WHAT IF SHE'S OUT THERE, SCARED AND ALONE, WHAT IF...
ANSWER!
COME ON! ANSWER YOUR PHONE!!
ERROR C4. THE CELLULAR NETWORK IS NOT AVAILABLE.
COME ON!!
JUST ANSWER YOUR PHONE.

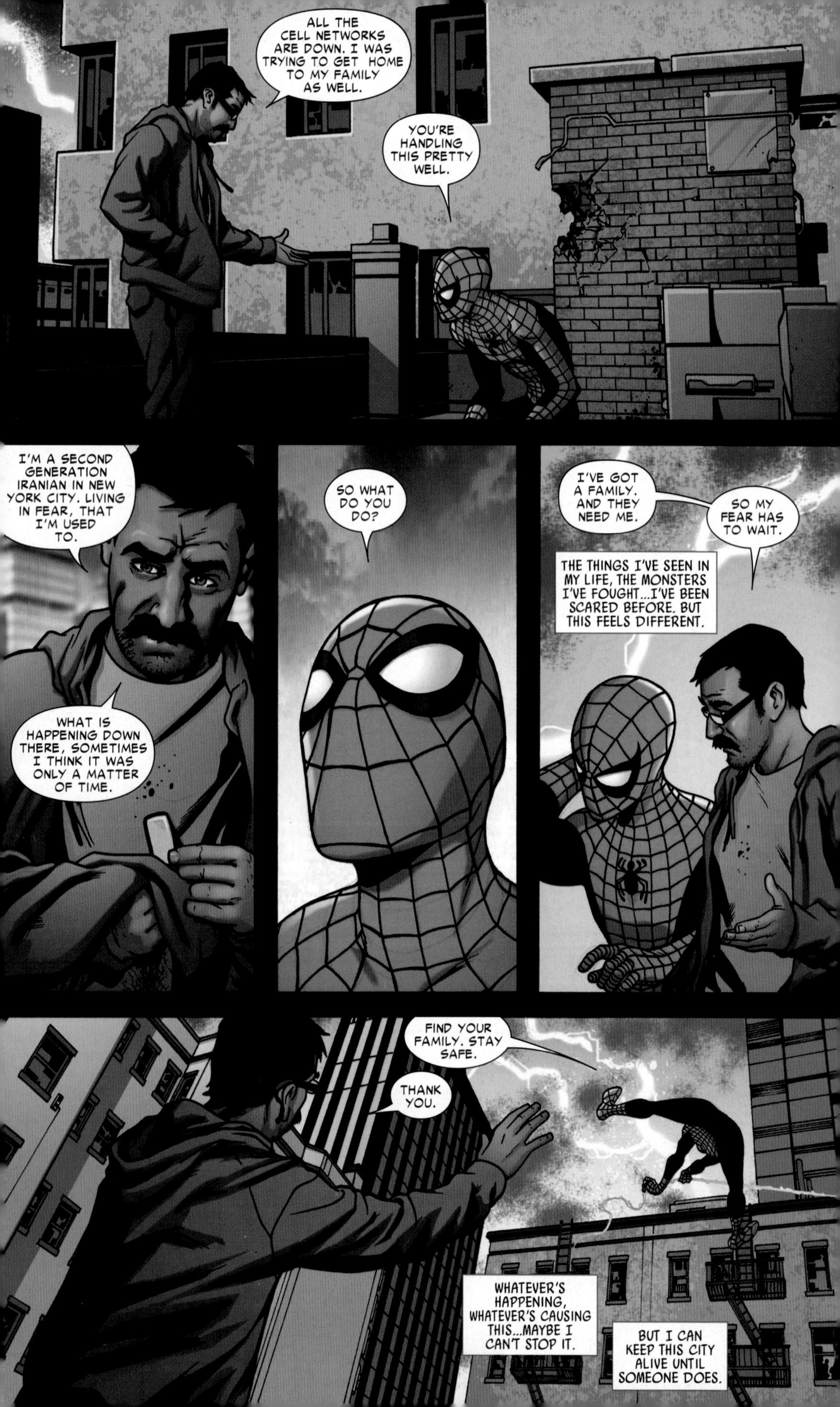

ALL THE CELL NETWORKS ARE DOWN. I WAS TRYING TO GET HOME TO MY FAMILY AS WELL.
YOU'RE HANDLING THIS PRETTY WELL.
I'M A SECOND GENERATION IRANIAN IN NEW YORK CITY. LIVING IN FEAR, THAT I'M USED TO.
WHAT IS HAPPENING DOWN THERE, SOMETIMES I THINK IT WAS ONLY A MATTER OF TIME.
SO WHAT DO YOU DO?
I'VE GOT A FAMILY. AND THEY NEED ME.
SO MY FEAR HAS TO WAIT.
THE THINGS I'VE SEEN IN MY LIFE, THE MONSTERS I'VE FOUGHT...I'VE BEEN SCARED BEFORE. BUT THIS FEELS DIFFERENT.
FIND YOUR FAMILY. STAY SAFE.
THANK YOU.
WHATEVER'S HAPPENING, WHATEVER'S CAUSING THIS...MAYBE I CAN'T STOP IT.
BUT I CAN KEEP THIS CITY ALIVE UNTIL SOMEONE DOES.

Hour Eleven of The Fear.

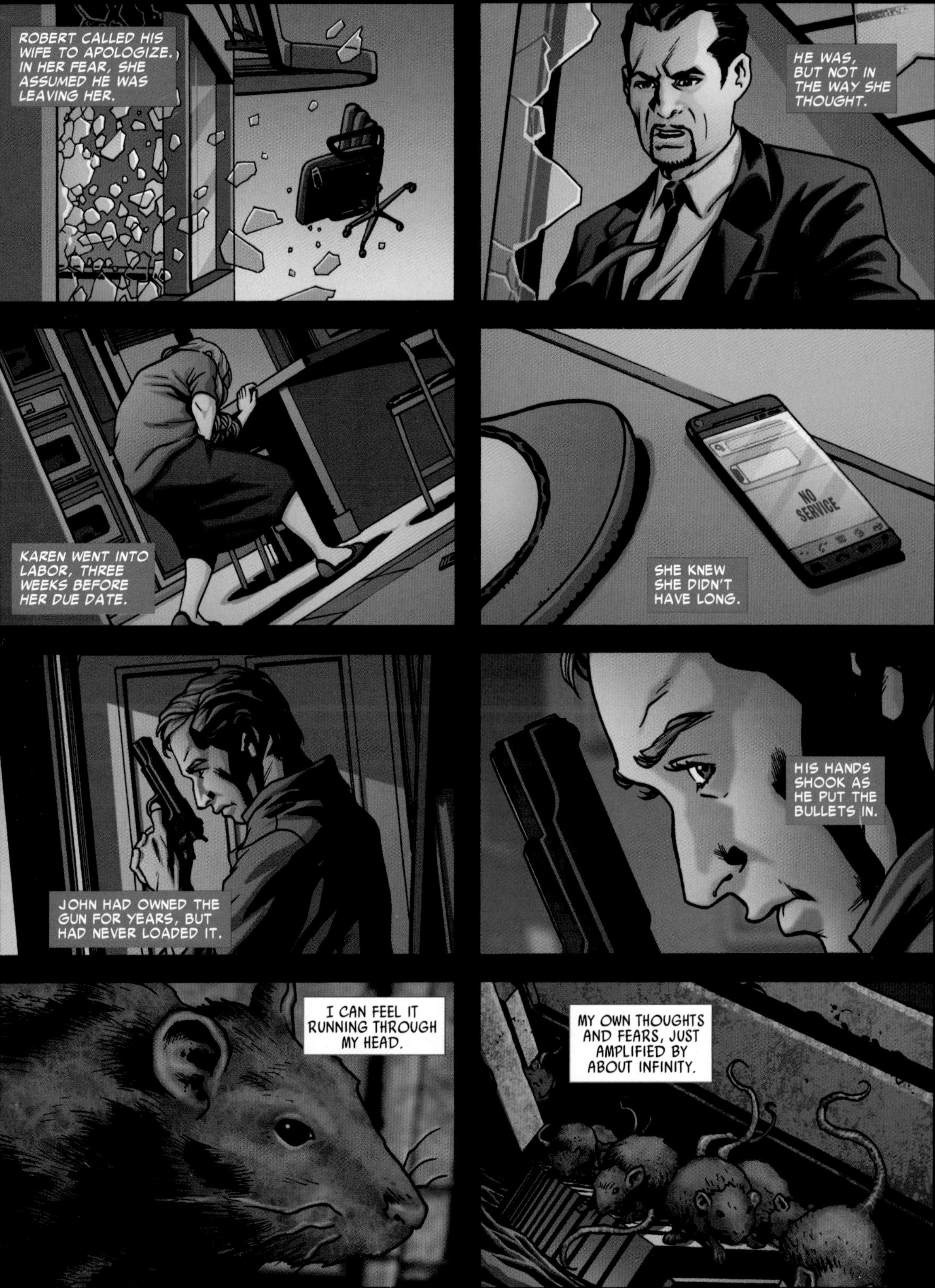
ROBERT CALLED HIS WIFE TO APOLOGIZE. IN HER FEAR, SHE ASSUMED HE WAS LEAVING HER.
HE WAS, BUT NOT IN THE WAY SHE THOUGHT.
KAREN WENT INTO LABOR, THREE WEEKS BEFORE HER DUE DATE.
NO SERVICE
SHE KNEW SHE DIDN'T HAVE LONG.
JOHN HAD OWNED THE GUN FOR YEARS, BUT HAD NEVER LOADED IT.
HIS HANDS SHOOK AS HE PUT THE BULLETS IN.
I CAN FEEL IT RUNNING THROUGH MY HEAD.
MY OWN THOUGHTS AND FEARS, JUST AMPLIFIED BY ABOUT INFINITY.

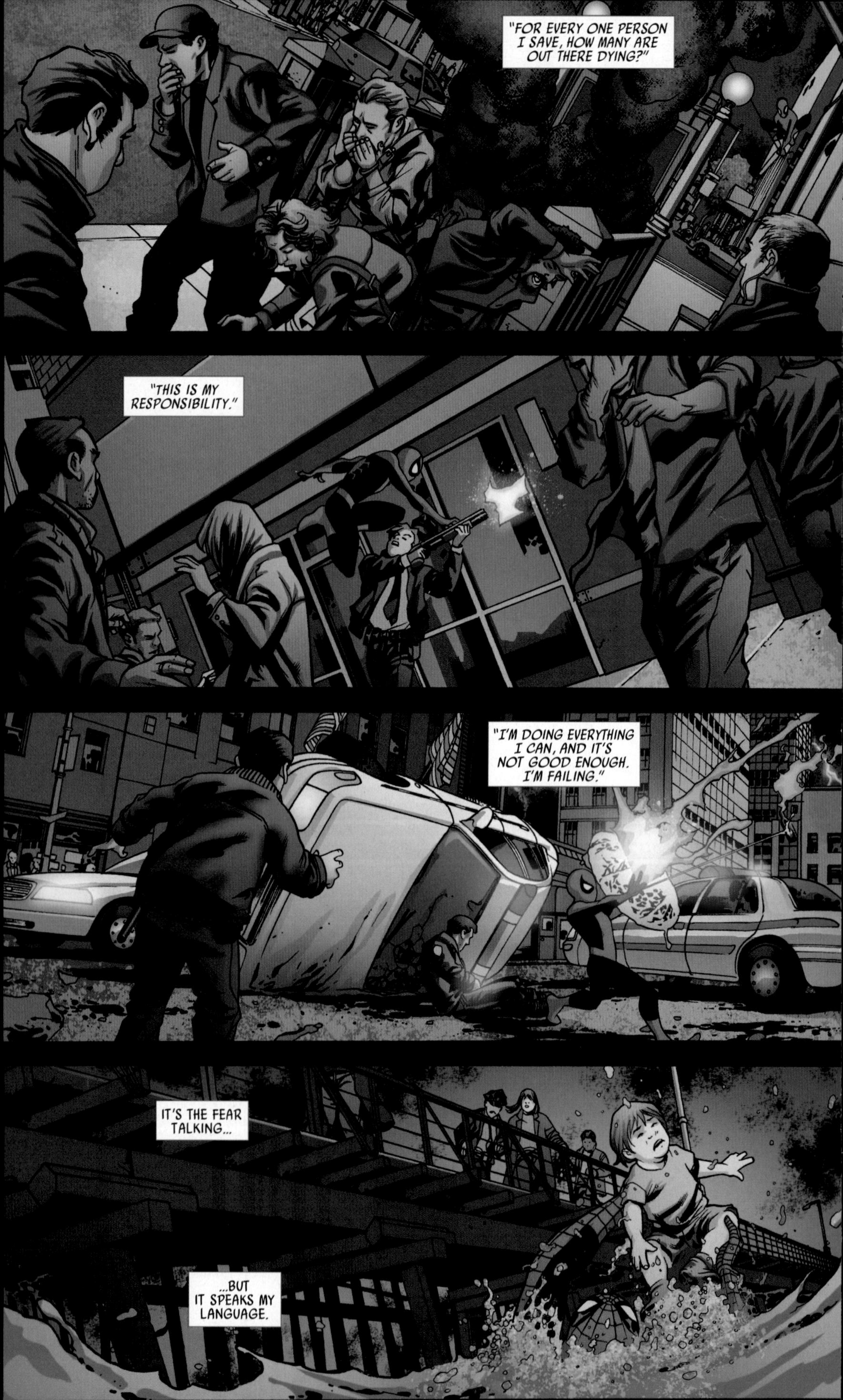
"FOR EVERY ONE PERSON I SAVE, HOW MANY ARE OUT THERE DYING?"
"THIS IS MY RESPONSIBILITY."
"I'M DOING EVERYTHING I CAN, AND IT'S NOT GOOD ENOUGH. I'M FAILING."
IT'S THE FEAR TALKING...
...BUT IT SPEAKS MY LANGUAGE.

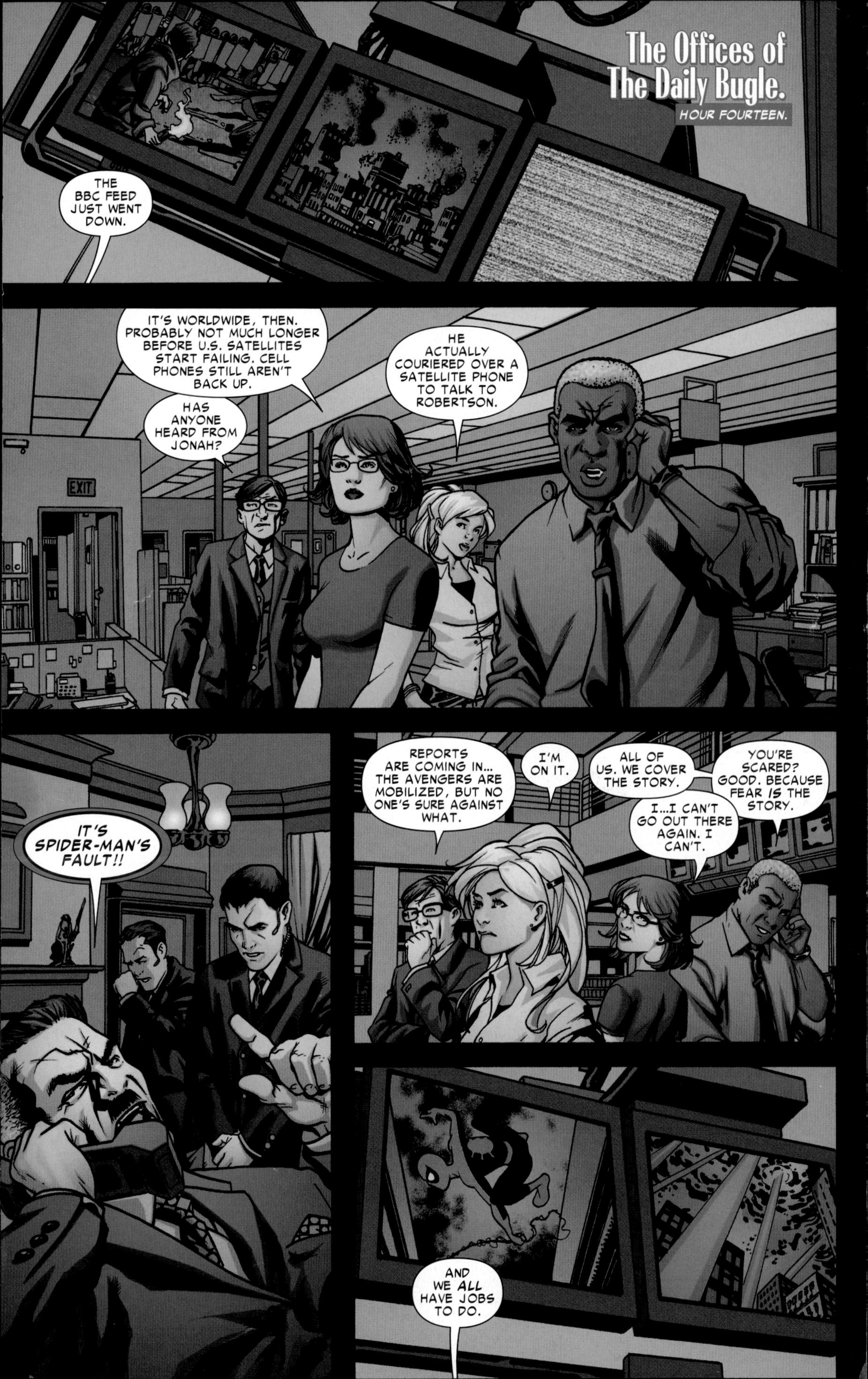
The Offices of The Daily Bugle.
HOUR FOURTEEN.
THE BBC FEED JUST WENT DOWN.
IT'S WORLDWIDE, THEN. PROBABLY NOT MUCH LONGER BEFORE U.S. SATELLITES START FAILING. CELL PHONES STILL AREN'T BACK UP.
HAS ANYONE HEARD FROM JONAH?
HE ACTUALLY COURIERED OVER A SATELLITE PHONE TO TALK TO ROBERTSON.
EXIT
IT'S SPIDER-MAN'S FAULT!!
REPORTS ARE COMING IN... THE AVENGERS ARE MOBILIZED, BUT NO ONE'S SURE AGAINST WHAT.
I'M ON IT.
ALL OF US. WE COVER THE STORY.
I...I CAN'T GO OUT THERE AGAIN. I CAN'T.
YOU'RE SCARED? GOOD. BECAUSE FEAR IS THE STORY.
AND WE ALL HAVE JOBS TO DO.

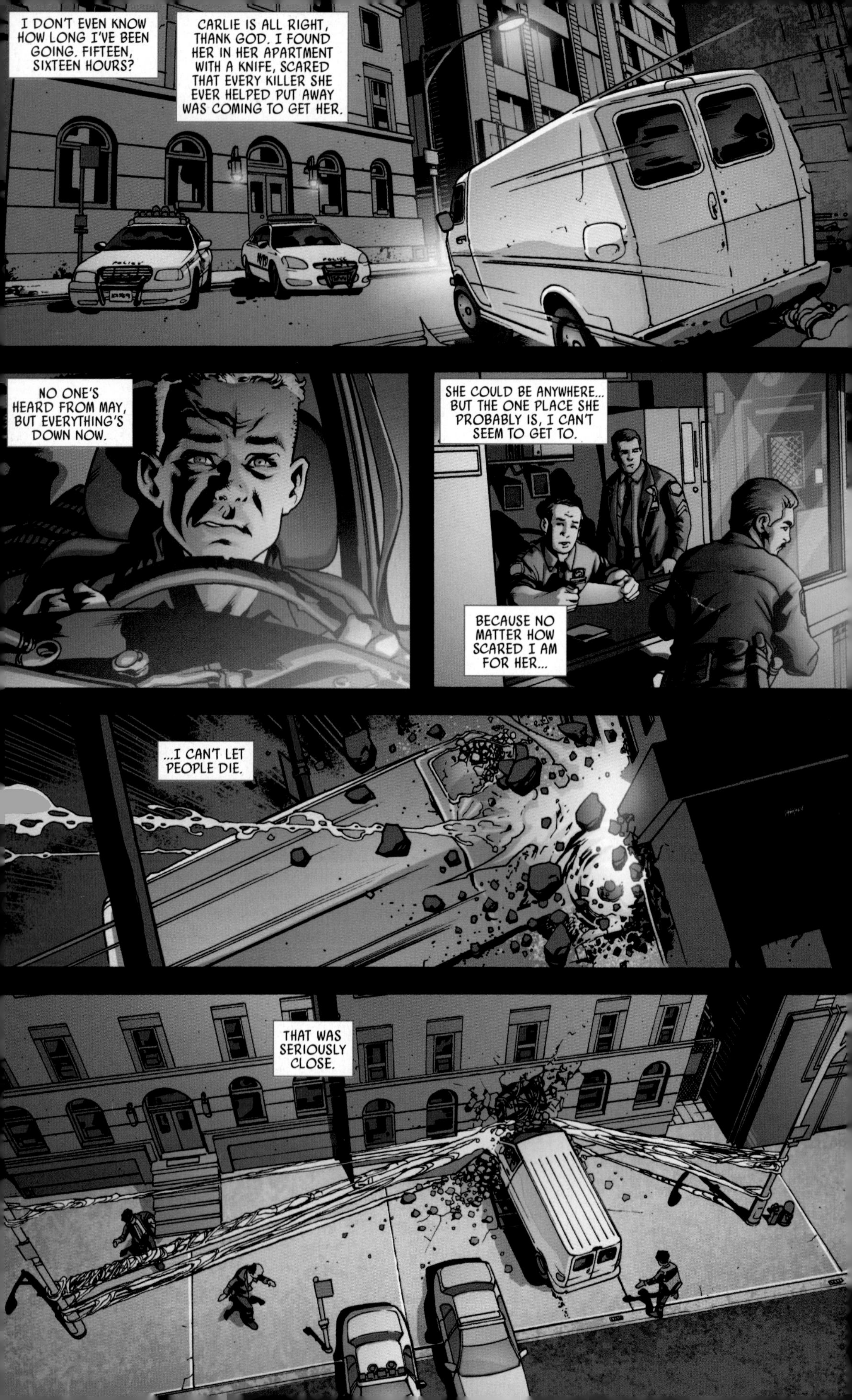
I DON'T EVEN KNOW HOW LONG I'VE BEEN GOING. FIFTEEN, SIXTEEN HOURS?
CARLIE IS ALL RIGHT, THANK GOD. I FOUND HER IN HER APARTMENT WITH A KNIFE, SCARED THAT EVERY KILLER SHE EVER HELPED PUT AWAY WAS COMING TO GET HER.
NO ONE'S HEARD FROM MAY, BUT EVERYTHING'S DOWN NOW.
SHE COULD BE ANYWHERE... BUT THE ONE PLACE SHE PROBABLY IS, I CAN'T SEEM TO GET TO.
BECAUSE NO MATTER HOW SCARED I AM FOR HER...
...I CAN'T LET PEOPLE DIE.
THAT WAS SERIOUSLY CLOSE.

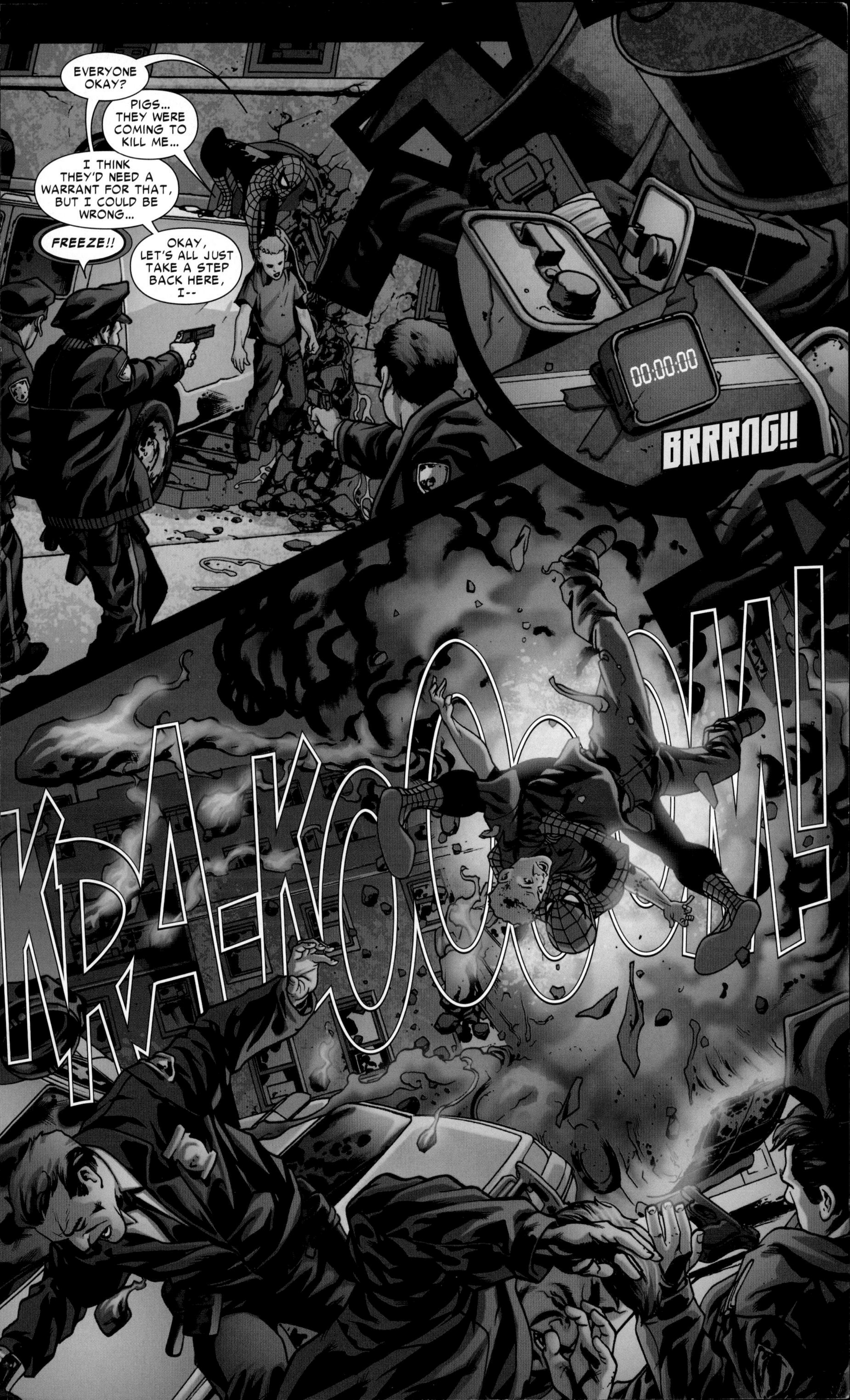

EVERYONE OKAY?
PIGS... THEY WERE COMING TO KILL ME...
I THINK THEY'D NEED A WARRANT FOR THAT, BUT I COULD BE WRONG...
FREEZE!!
OKAY, LET'S ALL JUST TAKE A STEP BACK HERE, I--
00:00:00
BRRRNG!!
KRA-KOOOOOM!!

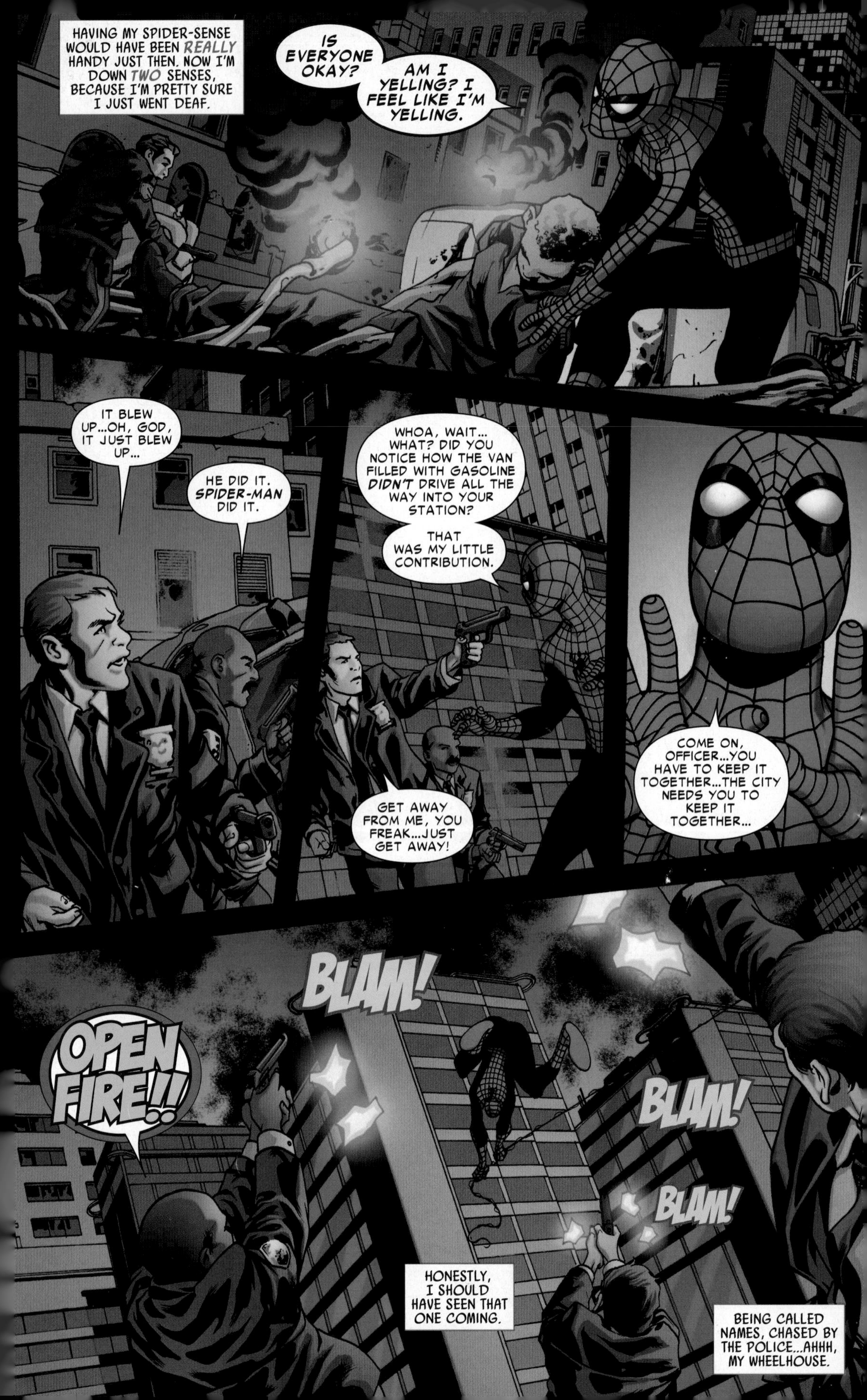
HAVING MY SPIDER-SENSE WOULD HAVE BEEN REALLY HANDY JUST THEN. NOW I'M DOWN TWO SENSES, BECAUSE I'M PRETTY SURE I JUST WENT DEAF.
IS EVERYONE OKAY?
AM I YELLING? I FEEL LIKE I'M YELLING.
IT BLEW UP...OH, GOD, IT JUST BLEW UP...
HE DID IT. SPIDER-MAN DID IT.
WHOA, WAIT... WHAT? DID YOU NOTICE HOW THE VAN FILLED WITH GASOLINE DIDN'T DRIVE ALL THE WAY INTO YOUR STATION?
THAT WAS MY LITTLE CONTRIBUTION.
GET AWAY FROM ME, YOU FREAK...JUST GET AWAY!
COME ON, OFFICER...YOU HAVE TO KEEP IT TOGETHER...THE CITY NEEDS YOU TO KEEP IT TOGETHER...
OPEN FIRE!!
BLAM!
BLAM!
BLAM!
HONESTLY, I SHOULD HAVE SEEN THAT ONE COMING.
BEING CALLED NAMES, CHASED BY THE POLICE...AHHH, MY WHEELHOUSE.

Hour Twenty of The Fear.

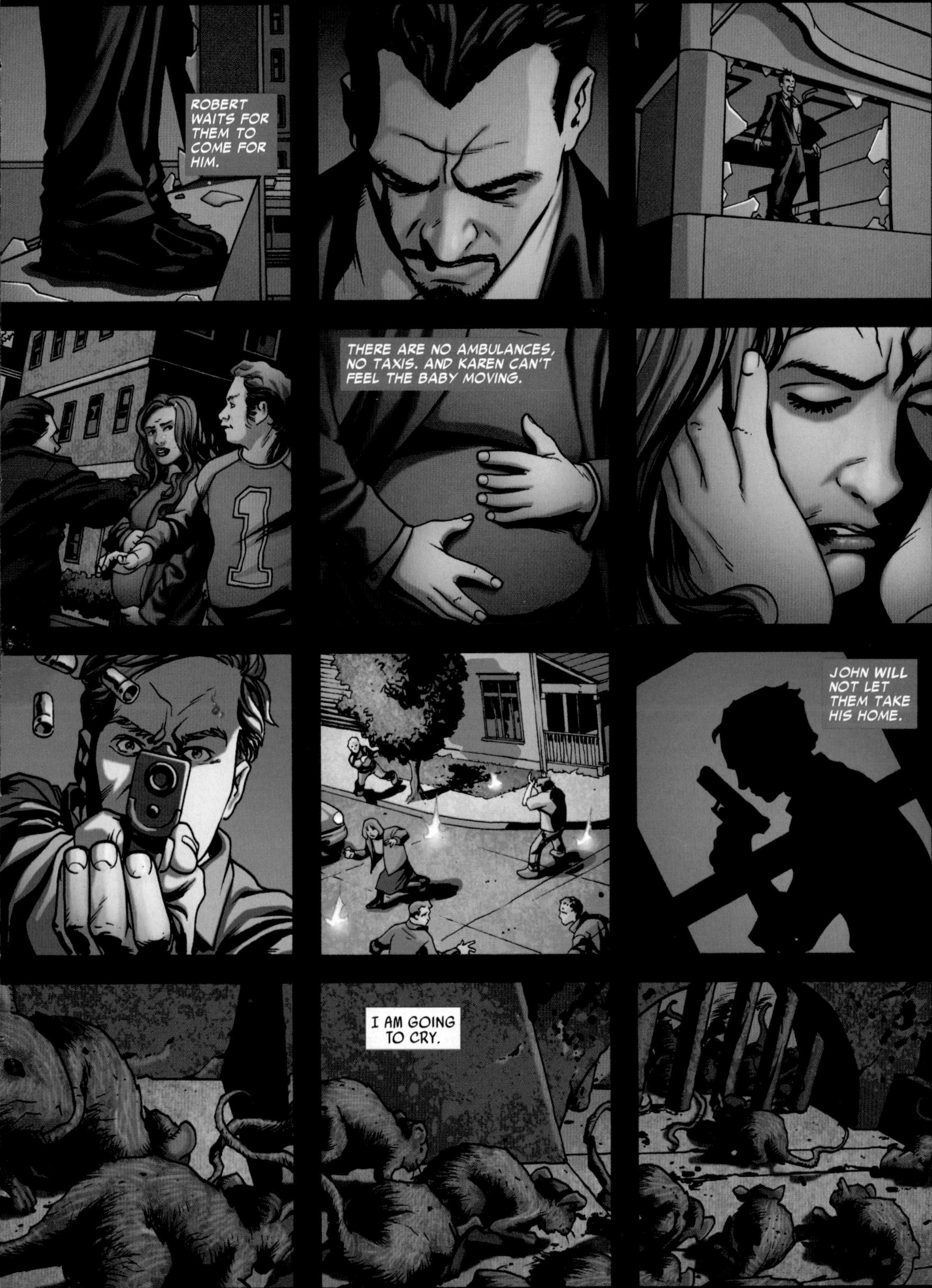
ROBERT WAITS FOR THEM TO COME FOR HIM.
THERE ARE NO AMBULANCES, NO TAXIS. AND KAREN CAN'T FEEL THE BABY MOVING.
JOHN WILL NOT LET THEM TAKE HIS HOME.
I AM GOING TO CRY.

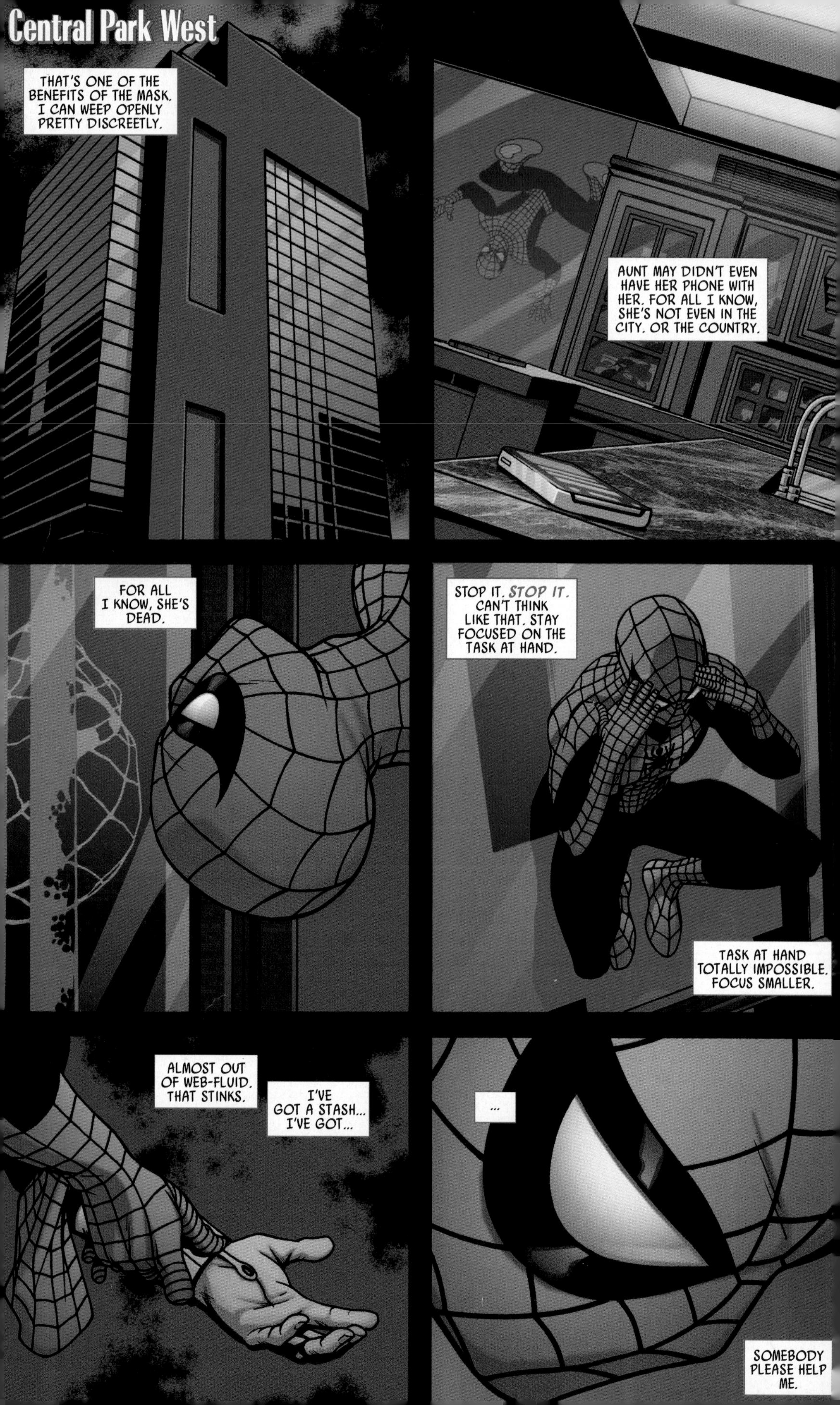

Central Park West
THAT'S ONE OF THE BENEFITS OF THE MASK. I CAN WEEP OPENLY PRETTY DISCREETLY.
AUNT MAY DIDN'T EVEN HAVE HER PHONE WITH HER. FOR ALL I KNOW, SHE'S NOT EVEN IN THE CITY. OR THE COUNTRY.
FOR ALL I KNOW, SHE'S DEAD.
STOP IT. *STOP IT.* CAN'T THINK LIKE THAT. STAY FOCUSED ON THE TASK AT HAND.
TASK AT HAND TOTALLY IMPOSSIBLE. FOCUS SMALLER.
ALMOST OUT OF WEB-FLUID. THAT STINKS.
I'VE GOT A STASH... I'VE GOT...
...
SOMEBODY PLEASE HELP ME.

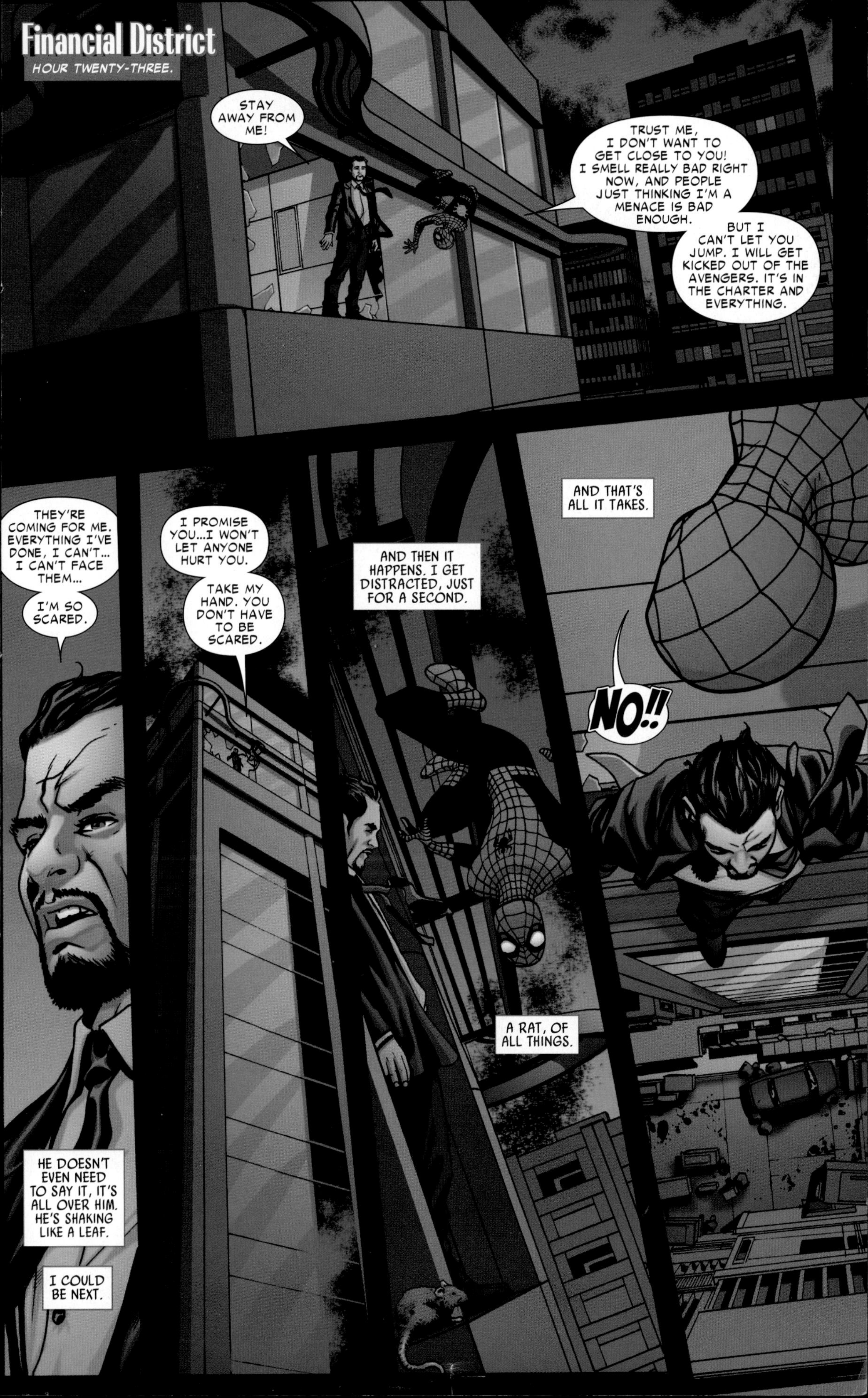
Financial District
HOUR TWENTY-THREE.
STAY AWAY FROM ME!
TRUST ME, I DON'T WANT TO GET CLOSE TO YOU! I SMELL REALLY BAD RIGHT NOW, AND PEOPLE JUST THINKING I'M A MENACE IS BAD ENOUGH.
BUT I CAN'T LET YOU JUMP. I WILL GET KICKED OUT OF THE AVENGERS. IT'S IN THE CHARTER AND EVERYTHING.
THEY'RE COMING FOR ME. EVERYTHING I'VE DONE, I CAN'T... I CAN'T FACE THEM...
I'M SO SCARED.
HE DOESN'T EVEN NEED TO SAY IT, IT'S ALL OVER HIM. HE'S SHAKING LIKE A LEAF.
I COULD BE NEXT.
I PROMISE YOU...I WON'T LET ANYONE HURT YOU.
TAKE MY HAND. YOU DON'T HAVE TO BE SCARED.
AND THEN IT HAPPENS. I GET DISTRACTED, JUST FOR A SECOND.
A RAT, OF ALL THINGS.
AND THAT'S ALL IT TAKES.
NO!!

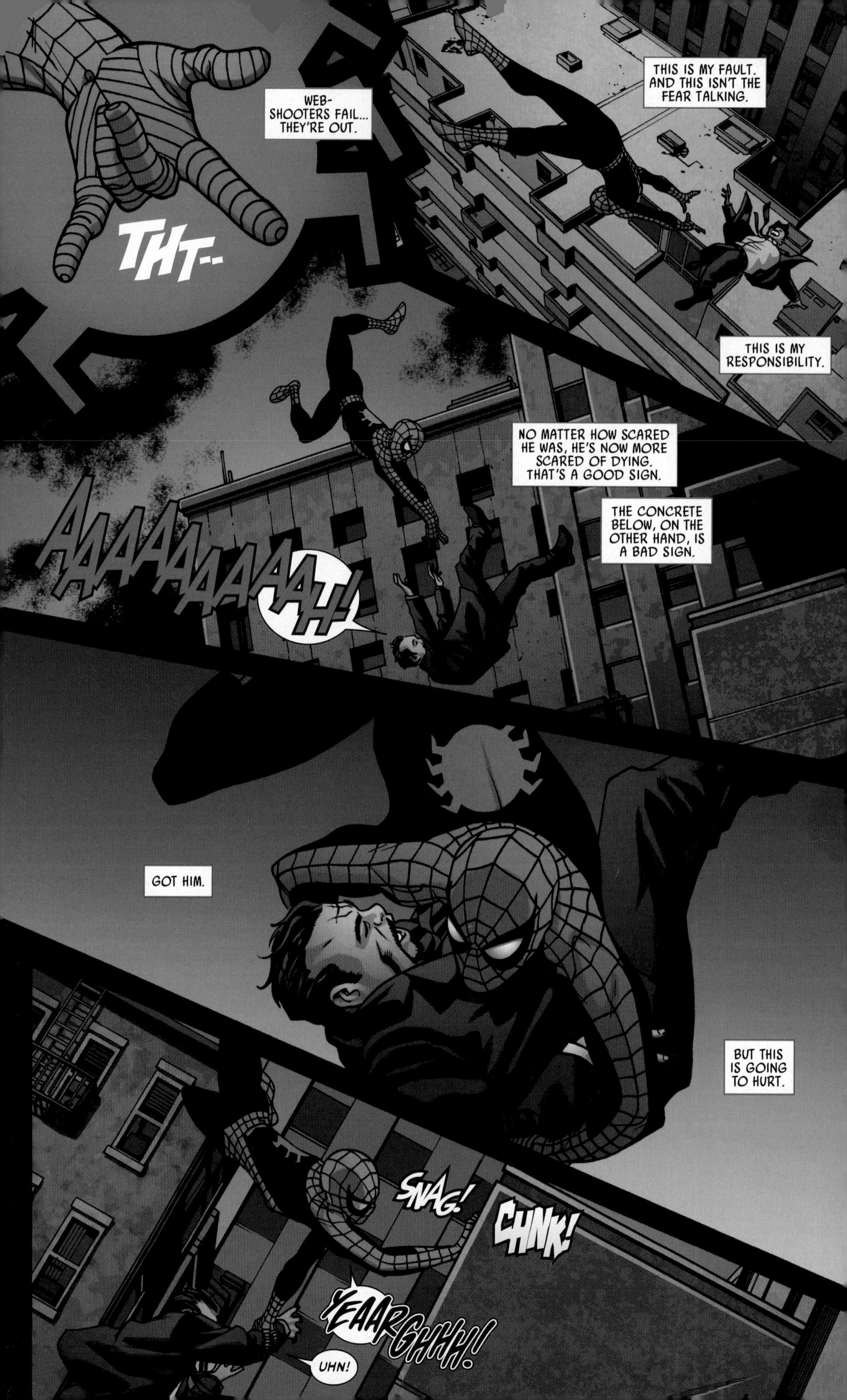
WEB-SHOOTERS FAIL... THEY'RE OUT.
THT--
THIS IS MY FAULT. AND THIS ISN'T THE FEAR TALKING.
THIS IS MY RESPONSIBILITY.
NO MATTER HOW SCARED HE WAS, HE'S NOW MORE SCARED OF DYING. THAT'S A GOOD SIGN.
THE CONCRETE BELOW, ON THE OTHER HAND, IS A BAD SIGN.
AAAAAAAAAAAH!
GOT HIM.
BUT THIS IS GOING TO HURT.
SNAG!
CHNK!
YEAARGHHH!
UHN!

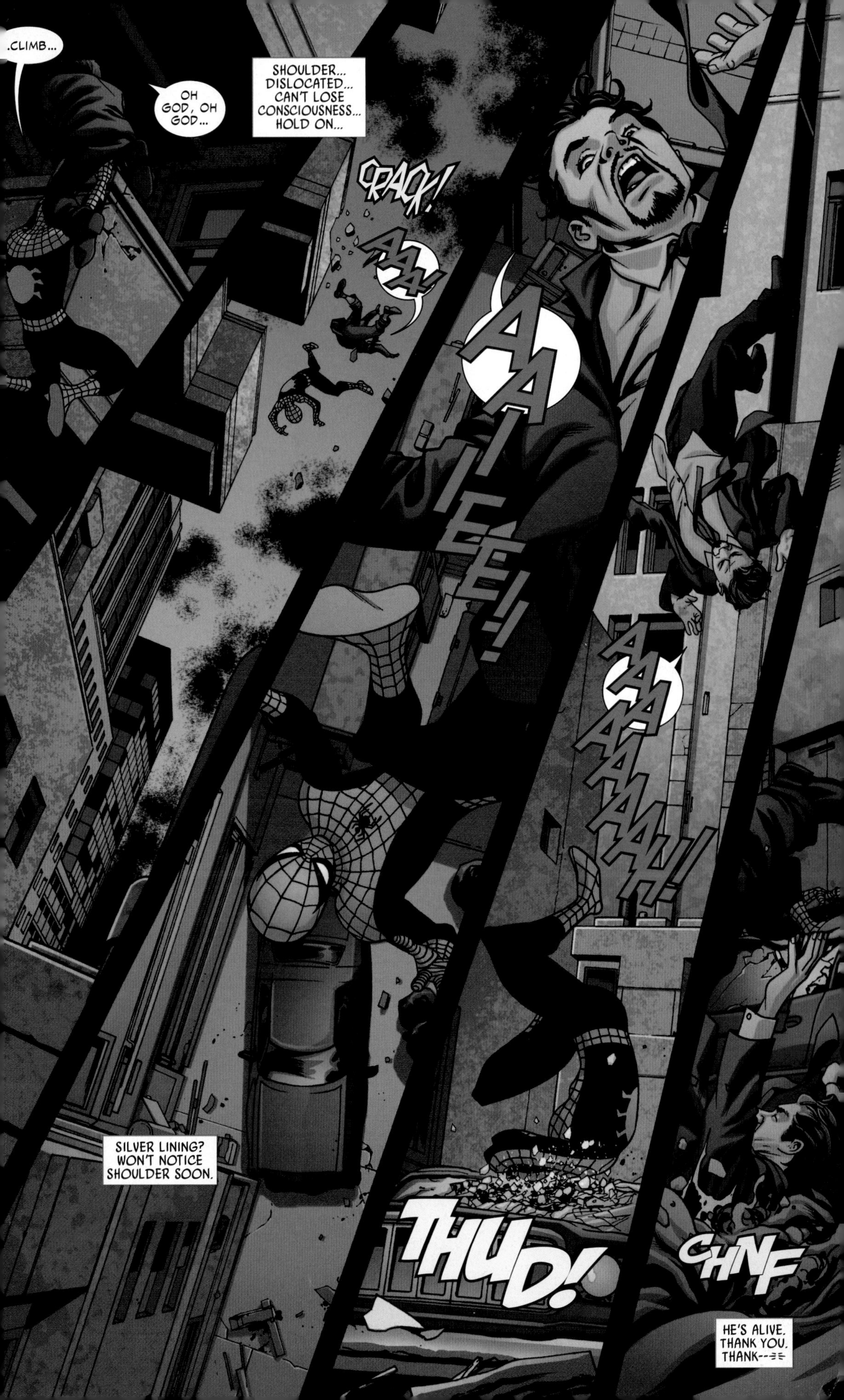
.CLIMB...
OH GOD, OH GOD...
SHOULDER... DISLOCATED... CAN'T LOSE CONSCIOUSNESS... HOLD ON...
CRACK!
AAA!
AAIIEEE!!
AAAAAAAAH!
SILVER LINING? WON'T NOTICE SHOULDER SOON.
THUD!
CHNF
HE'S ALIVE. THANK YOU. THANK--

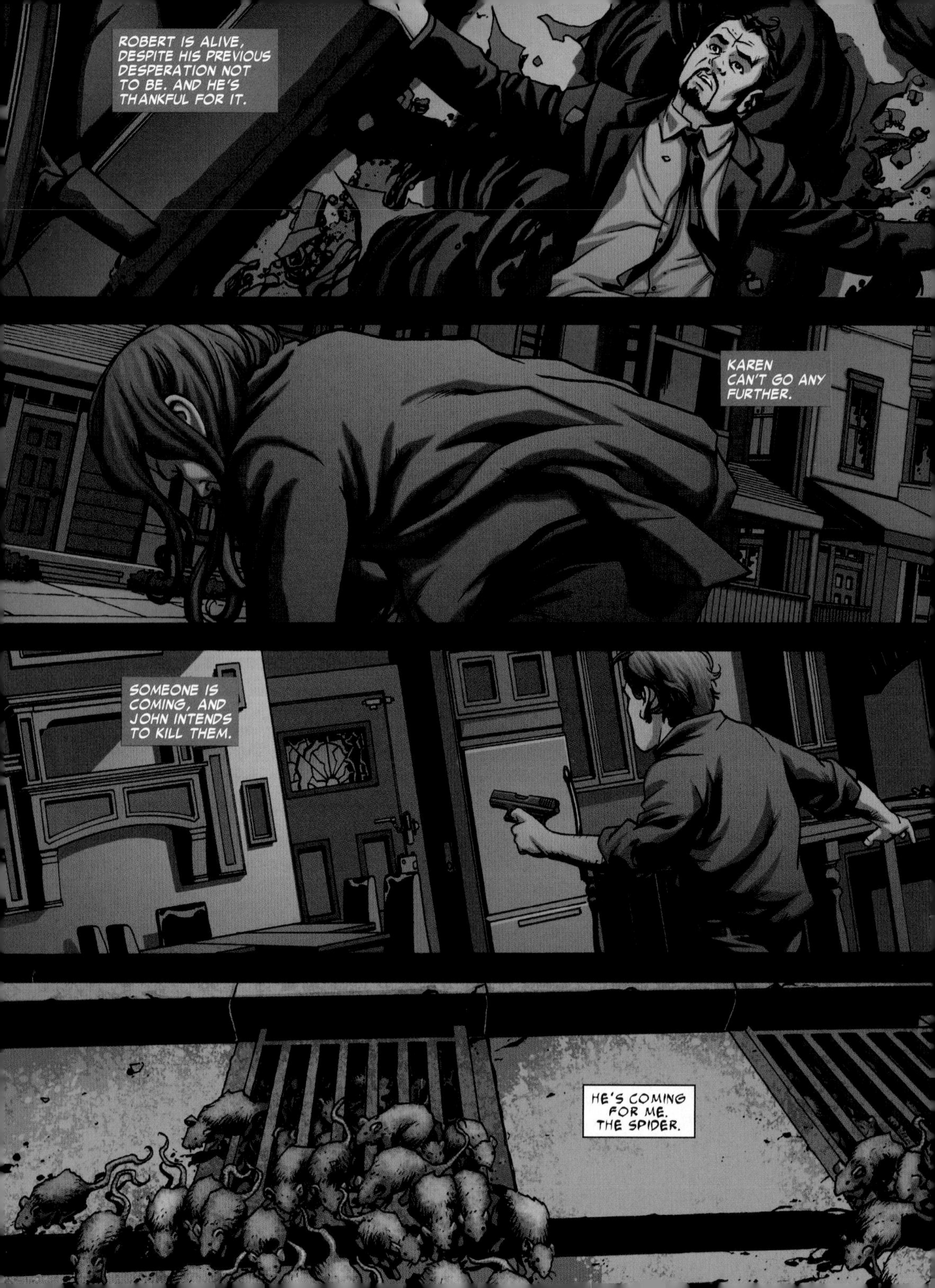
ROBERT IS ALIVE, DESPITE HIS PREVIOUS DESPERATION NOT TO BE. AND HE'S THANKFUL FOR IT.
KAREN CAN'T GO ANY FURTHER.
SOMEONE IS COMING, AND JOHN INTENDS TO KILL THEM.
HE'S COMING FOR ME. THE SPIDER.

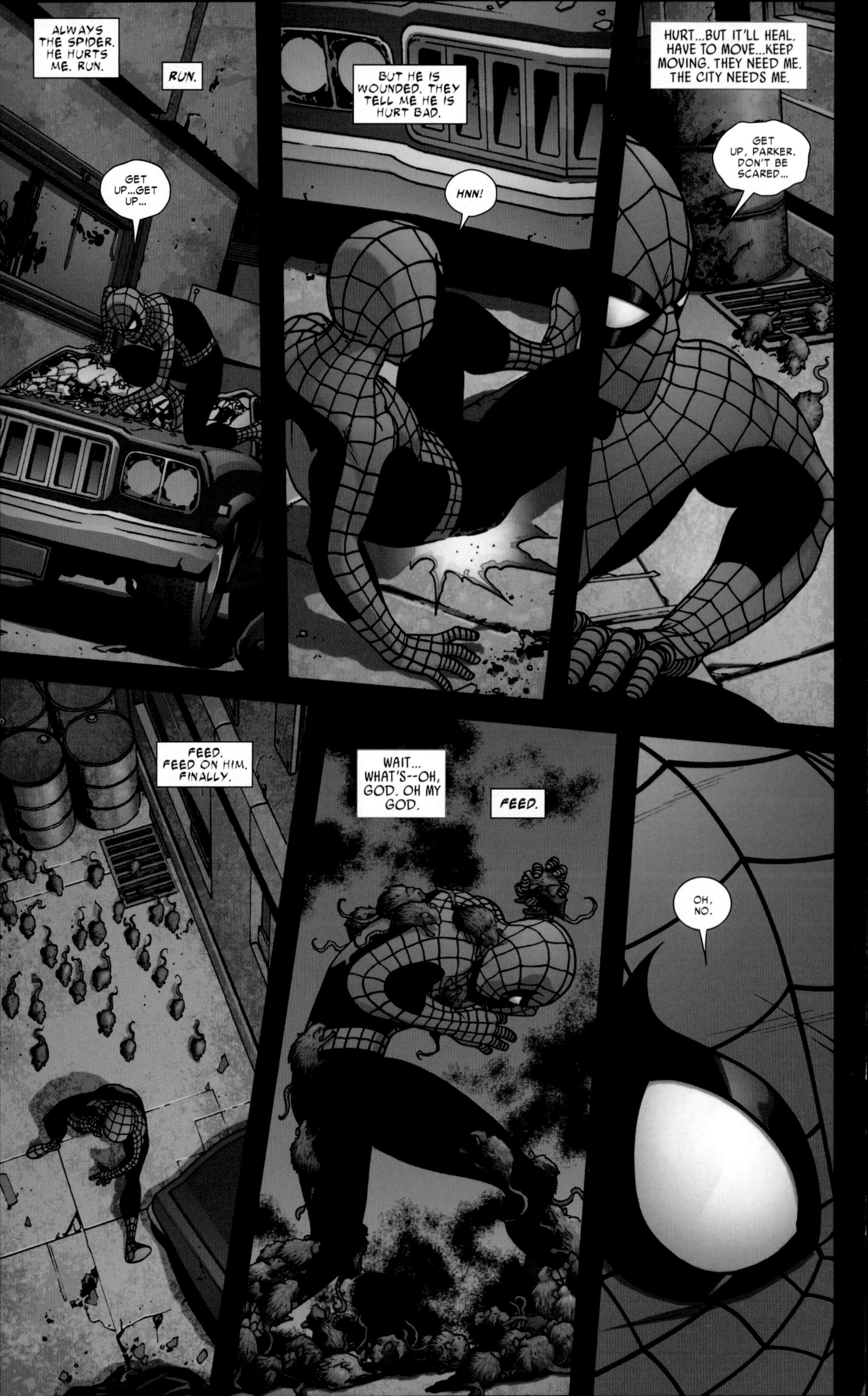
ALWAYS THE SPIDER. HE HURTS ME. RUN.
RUN.
GET UP...GET UP...
BUT HE IS WOUNDED. THEY TELL ME HE IS HURT BAD.
HNN!
HURT...BUT IT'LL HEAL. HAVE TO MOVE...KEEP MOVING. THEY NEED ME. THE CITY NEEDS ME.
GET UP, PARKER. DON'T BE SCARED...
FEED. FEED ON HIM. FINALLY.
WAIT... WHAT'S--OH, GOD. OH MY GOD.
FEED.
OH, NO.

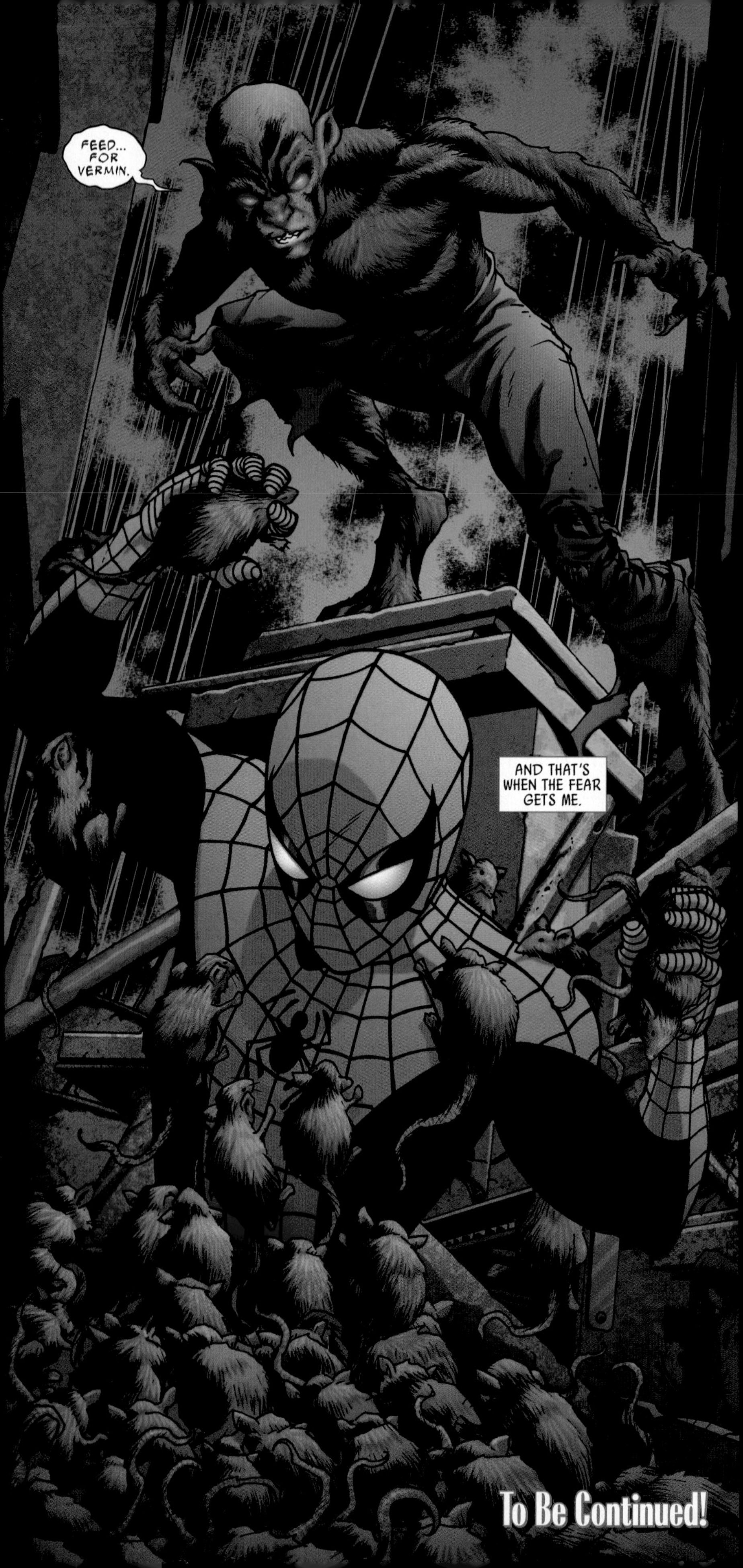
FEED... FOR VERMIN.
AND THAT'S WHEN THE FEAR GETS ME.
To Be Continued!

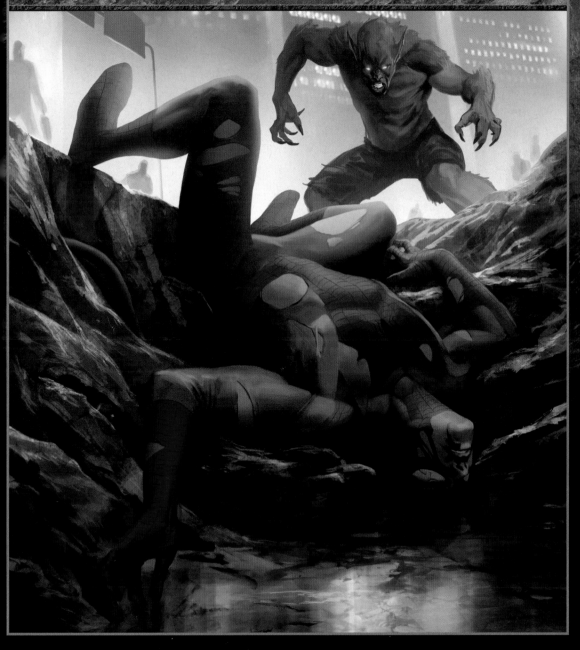

FEAR ITSELF
ITSELF
SPIDER-MAN

DAY TWO

Hour Twenty-Five Of The Fear.

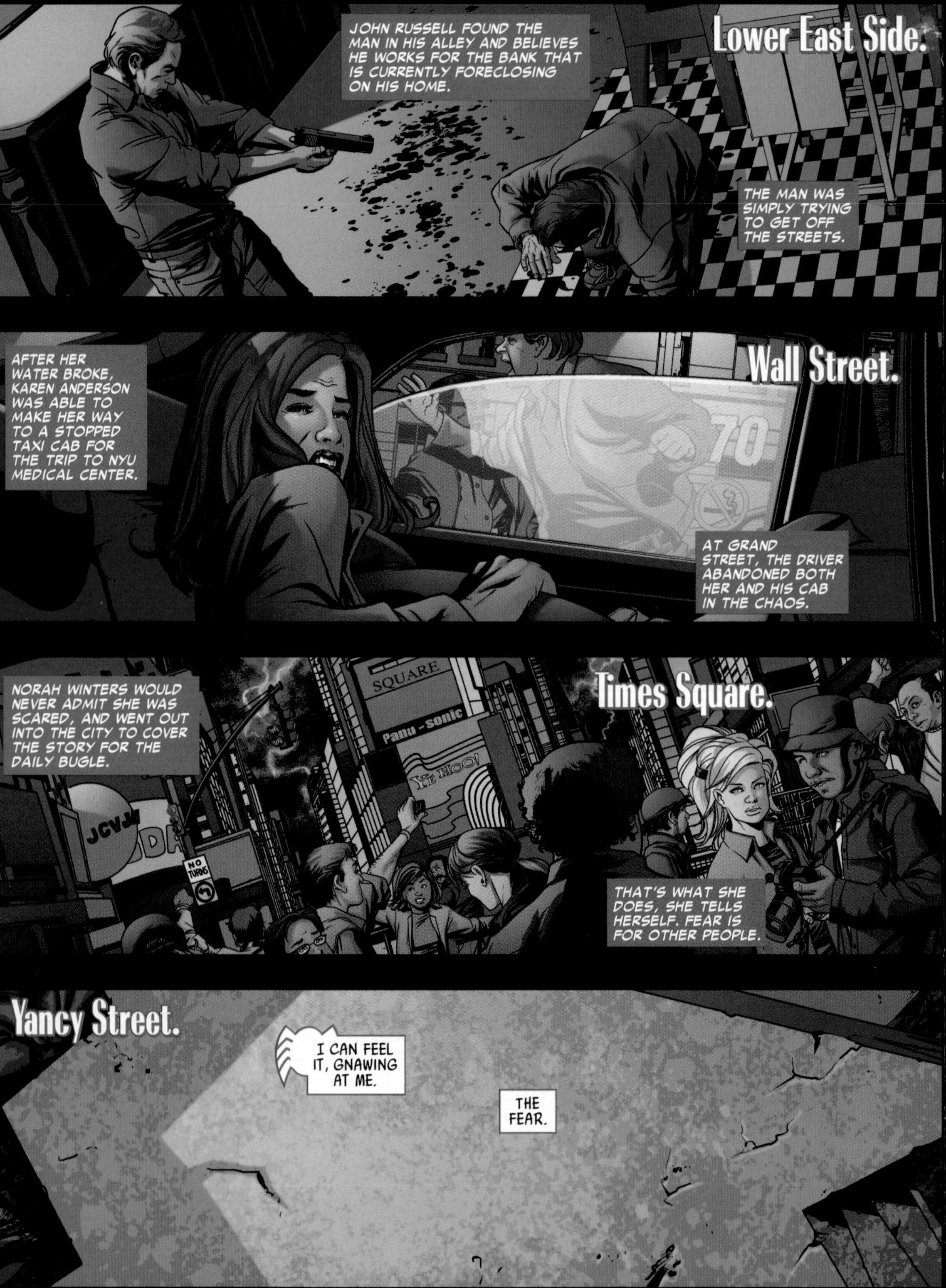
JOHN RUSSELL FOUND THE MAN IN HIS ALLEY AND BELIEVES HE WORKS FOR THE BANK THAT IS CURRENTLY FORECLOSING ON HIS HOME.
Lower East Side.
THE MAN WAS SIMPLY TRYING TO GET OFF THE STREETS.
AFTER HER WATER BROKE, KAREN ANDERSON WAS ABLE TO MAKE HER WAY TO A STOPPED TAXI CAB FOR THE TRIP TO NYU MEDICAL CENTER.
Wall Street.
AT GRAND STREET, THE DRIVER ABANDONED BOTH HER AND HIS CAB IN THE CHAOS.
NORAH WINTERS WOULD NEVER ADMIT SHE WAS SCARED, AND WENT OUT INTO THE CITY TO COVER THE STORY FOR THE DAILY BUGLE.
Times Square.
SQUARE
Panasonic
NO TURNS
THAT'S WHAT SHE DOES, SHE TELLS HERSELF. FEAR IS FOR OTHER PEOPLE.
Yancy Street.
I CAN FEEL IT, GNAWING AT ME.
THE FEAR.

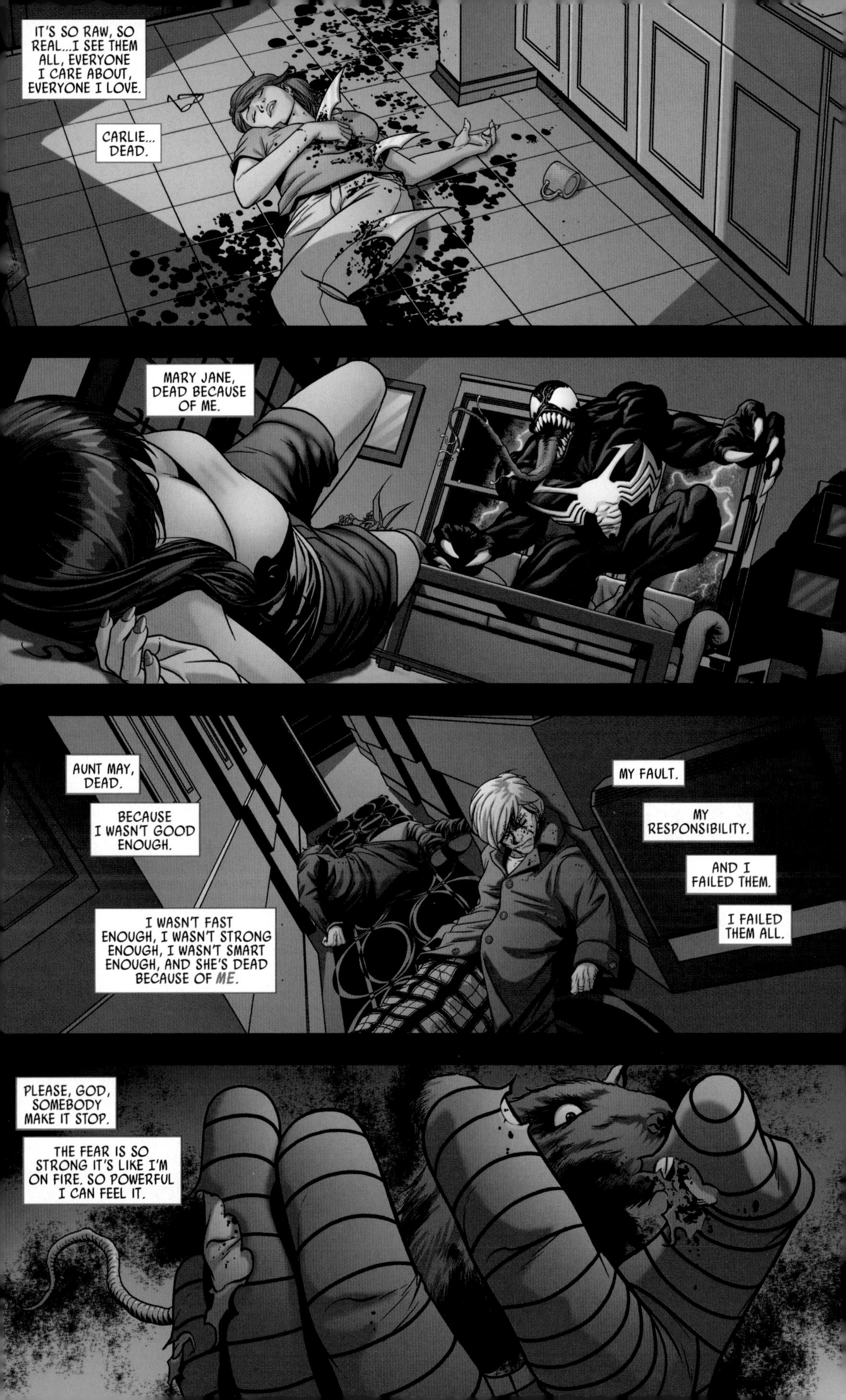
IT'S SO RAW, SO REAL...I SEE THEM ALL, EVERYONE I CARE ABOUT, EVERYONE I LOVE.
CARLIE... DEAD.
MARY JANE, DEAD BECAUSE OF ME.
AUNT MAY, DEAD.
BECAUSE I WASN'T GOOD ENOUGH.
I WASN'T FAST ENOUGH, I WASN'T STRONG ENOUGH, I WASN'T SMART ENOUGH, AND SHE'S DEAD BECAUSE OF ME.
MY FAULT.
MY RESPONSIBILITY.
AND I FAILED THEM.
I FAILED THEM ALL.
PLEASE, GOD, SOMEBODY MAKE IT STOP.
THE FEAR IS SO STRONG IT'S LIKE I'M ON FIRE. SO POWERFUL I CAN FEEL IT.

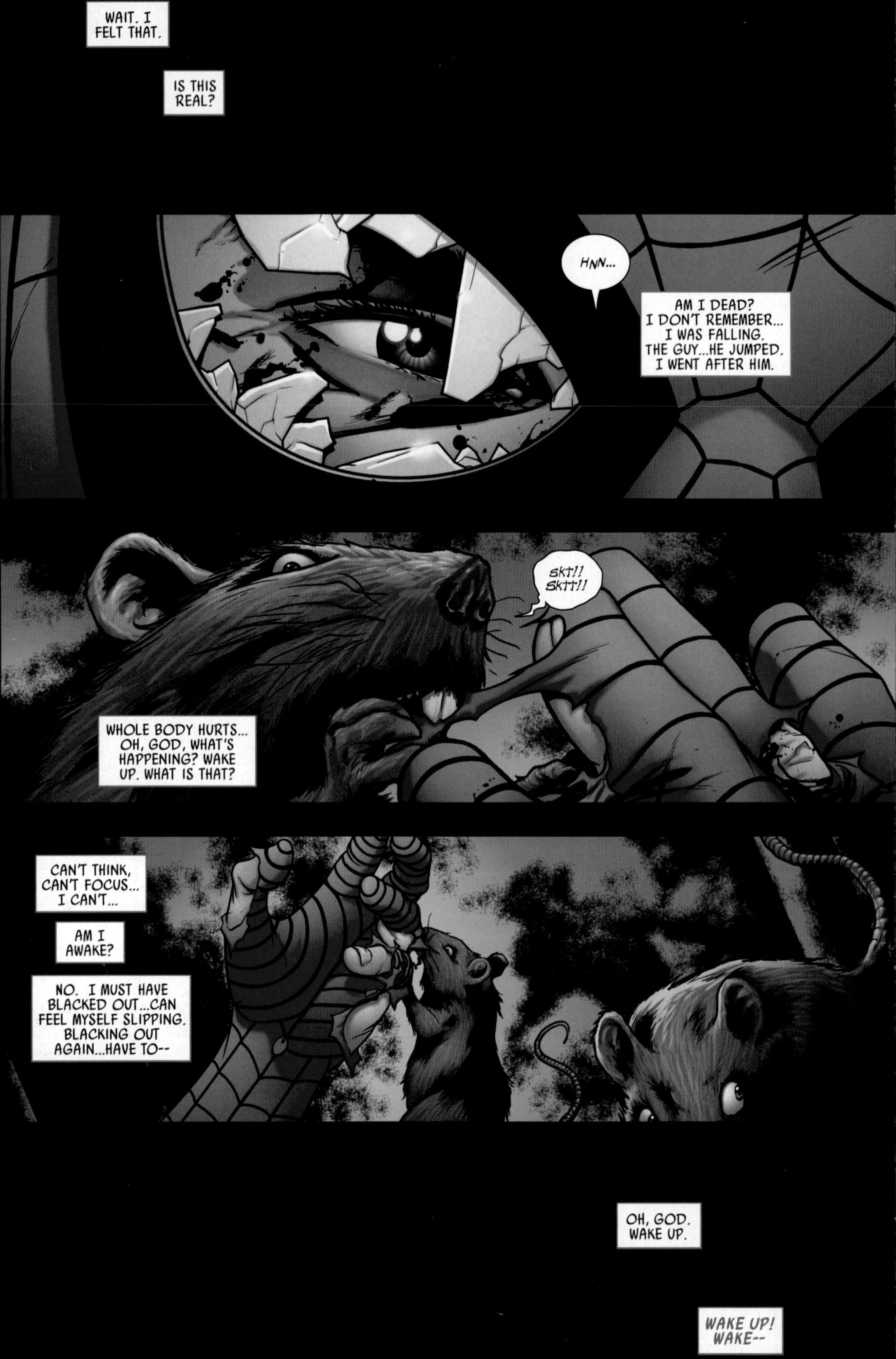
WAIT. I FELT THAT.
IS THIS REAL?
HNN...
AM I DEAD? I DON'T REMEMBER... I WAS FALLING. THE GUY...HE JUMPED. I WENT AFTER HIM.
SKT!! SKTT!!
WHOLE BODY HURTS... OH, GOD, WHAT'S HAPPENING? WAKE UP. WHAT IS THAT?
CAN'T THINK, CAN'T FOCUS... I CAN'T...
AM I AWAKE?
NO. I MUST HAVE BLACKED OUT...CAN FEEL MYSELF SLIPPING. BLACKING OUT AGAIN...HAVE TO--
OH, GOD. WAKE UP.
WAKE UP! WAKE--

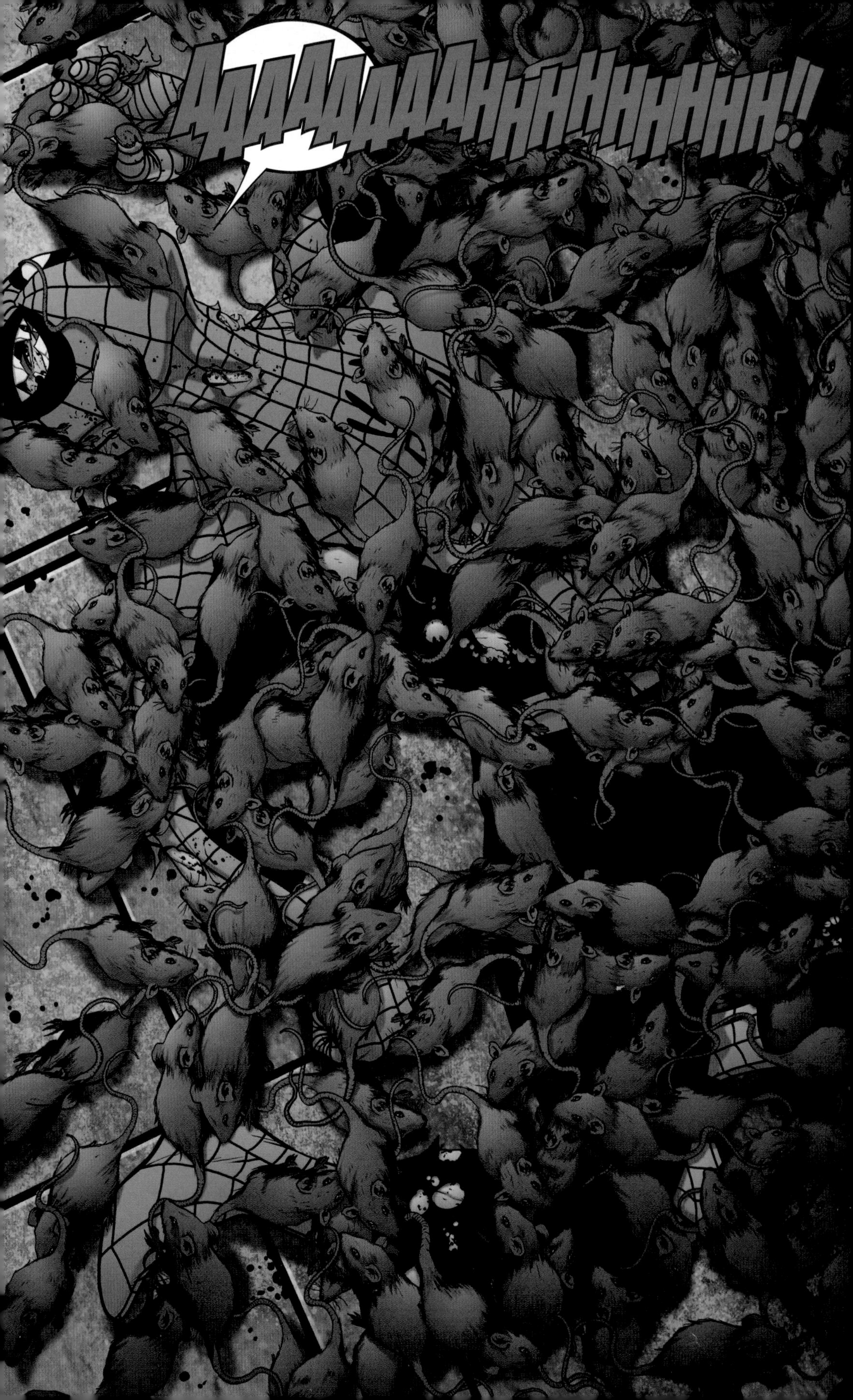
AAAAAAAHHHHHHHH!!

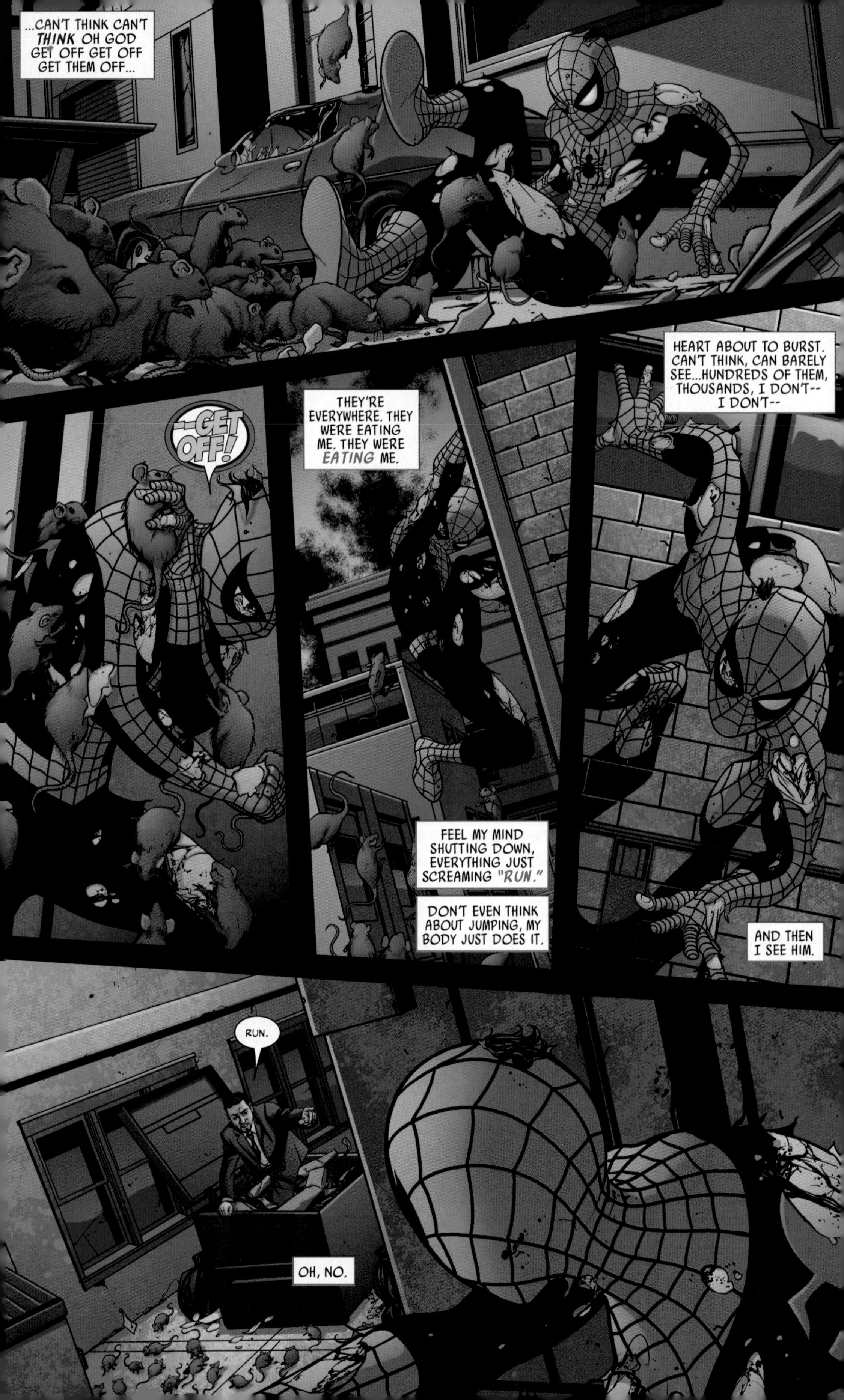
...CAN'T THINK CAN'T THINK OH GOD GET OFF GET OFF GET THEM OFF...
--GET OFF!
THEY'RE EVERYWHERE. THEY WERE EATING ME. THEY WERE EATING ME.
FEEL MY MIND SHUTTING DOWN, EVERYTHING JUST SCREAMING "RUN."
DON'T EVEN THINK ABOUT JUMPING, MY BODY JUST DOES IT.
HEART ABOUT TO BURST. CAN'T THINK, CAN BARELY SEE...HUNDREDS OF THEM, THOUSANDS, I DON'T-- I DON'T--
AND THEN I SEE HIM.
RUN.
OH, NO.

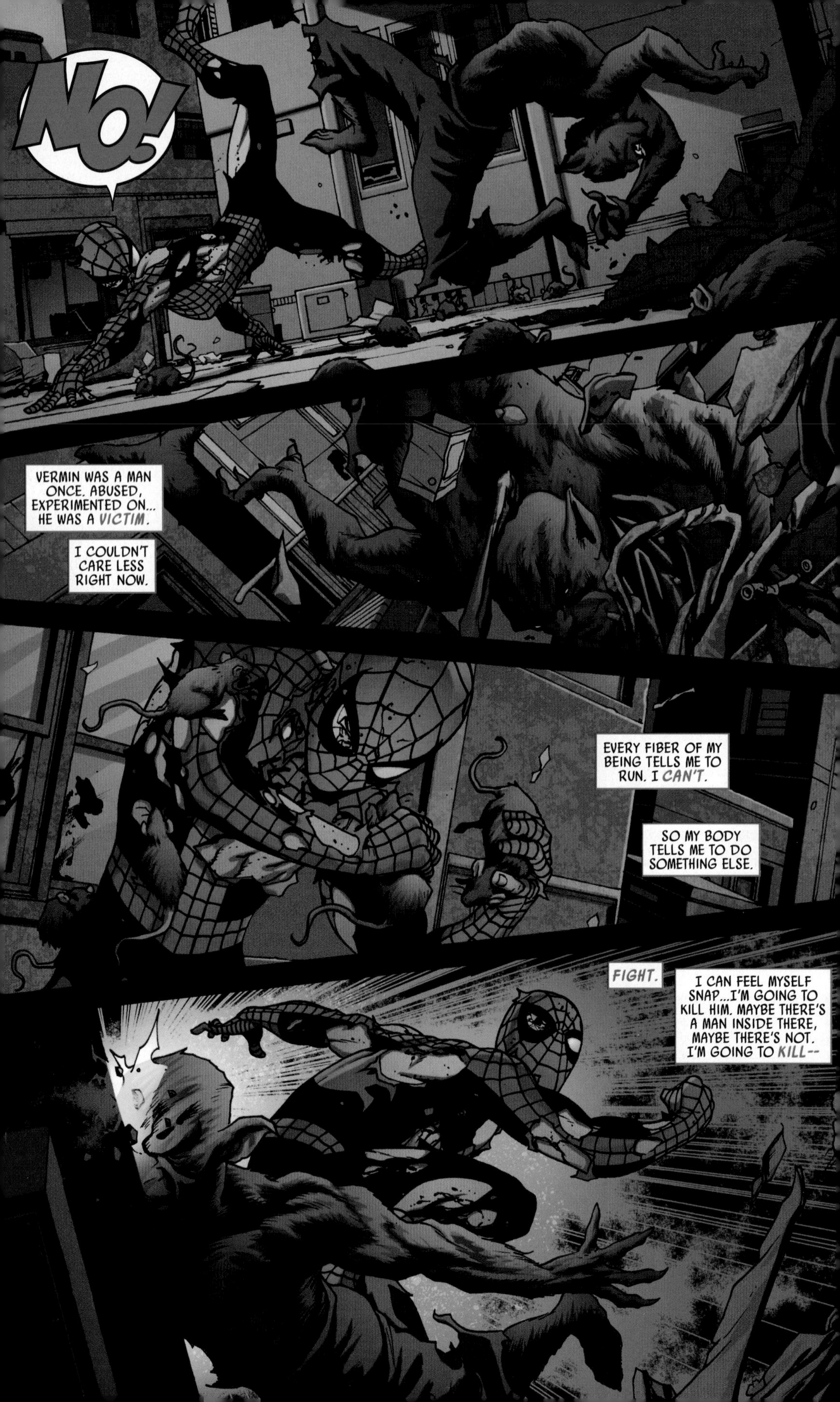
NO!
VERMIN WAS A MAN ONCE. ABUSED, EXPERIMENTED ON... HE WAS A VICTIM.
I COULDN'T CARE LESS RIGHT NOW.
EVERY FIBER OF MY BEING TELLS ME TO RUN. I CAN'T.
SO MY BODY TELLS ME TO DO SOMETHING ELSE.
FIGHT.
I CAN FEEL MYSELF SNAP...I'M GOING TO KILL HIM. MAYBE THERE'S A MAN INSIDE THERE, MAYBE THERE'S NOT. I'M GOING TO KILL--

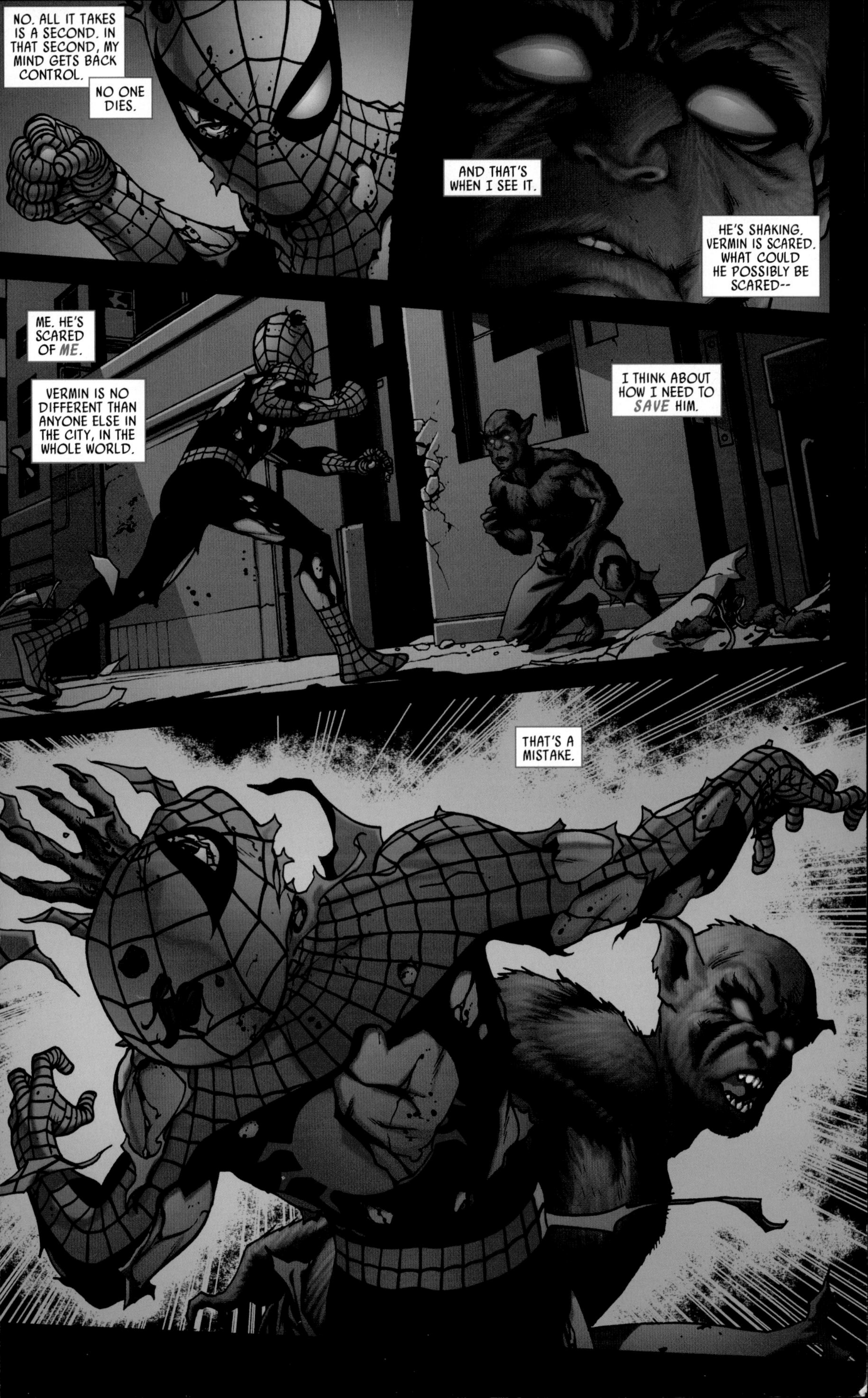
NO. ALL IT TAKES IS A SECOND. IN THAT SECOND, MY MIND GETS BACK CONTROL.
NO ONE DIES.
AND THAT'S WHEN I SEE IT.
HE'S SHAKING. VERMIN IS SCARED. WHAT COULD HE POSSIBLY BE SCARED--
ME. HE'S SCARED OF ME.
VERMIN IS NO DIFFERENT THAN ANYONE ELSE IN THE CITY, IN THE WHOLE WORLD.
I THINK ABOUT HOW I NEED TO SAVE HIM.
THAT'S A MISTAKE.

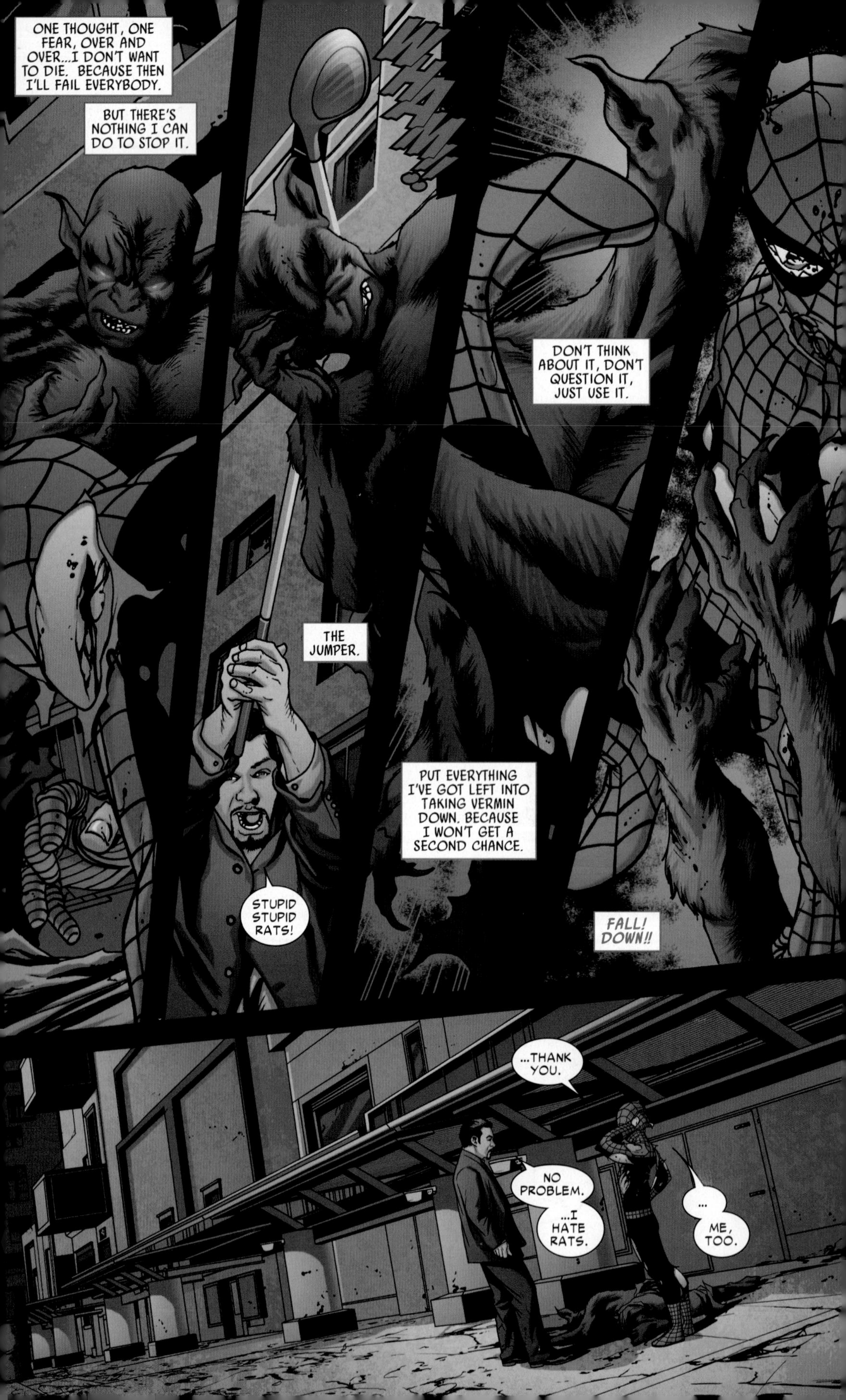
ONE THOUGHT, ONE FEAR, OVER AND OVER...I DON'T WANT TO DIE. BECAUSE THEN I'LL FAIL EVERYBODY.
BUT THERE'S NOTHING I CAN DO TO STOP IT.
WHAMM!
DON'T THINK ABOUT IT, DON'T QUESTION IT, JUST USE IT.
THE JUMPER.
PUT EVERYTHING I'VE GOT LEFT INTO TAKING VERMIN DOWN. BECAUSE I WON'T GET A SECOND CHANCE.
STUPID STUPID RATS!
FALL! DOWN!!
...THANK YOU.
NO PROBLEM.
...I HATE RATS.
...
ME, TOO.

Hour Twenty-Eight Of The Fear.

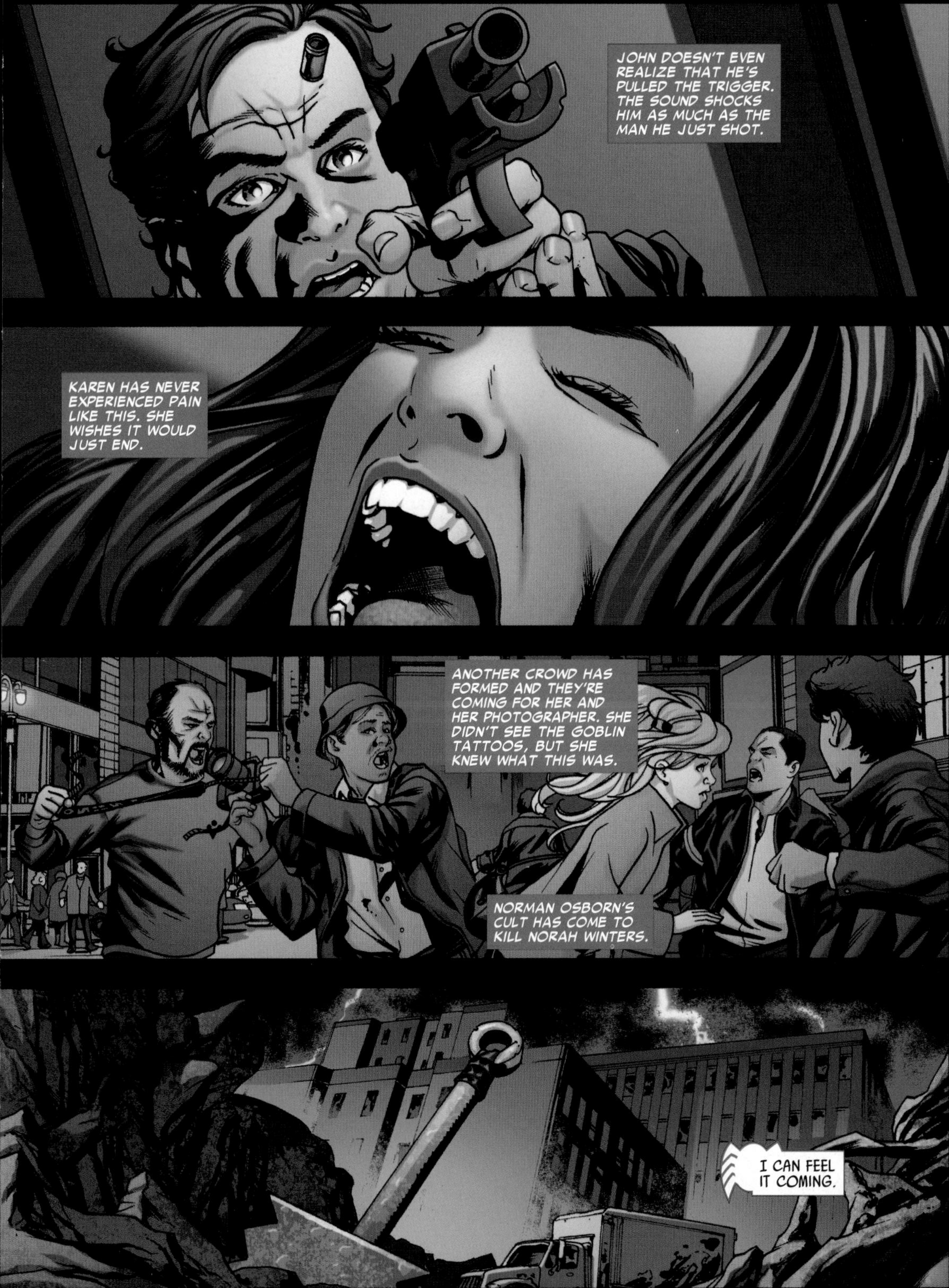

JOHN DOESN'T EVEN REALIZE THAT HE'S PULLED THE TRIGGER. THE SOUND SHOCKS HIM AS MUCH AS THE MAN HE JUST SHOT.
KAREN HAS NEVER EXPERIENCED PAIN LIKE THIS. SHE WISHES IT WOULD JUST END.
ANOTHER CROWD HAS FORMED AND THEY'RE COMING FOR HER AND HER PHOTOGRAPHER. SHE DIDN'T SEE THE GOBLIN TATTOOS, BUT SHE KNEW WHAT THIS WAS.
NORMAN OSBORN'S CULT HAS COME TO KILL NORAH WINTERS.
I CAN FEEL IT COMING.

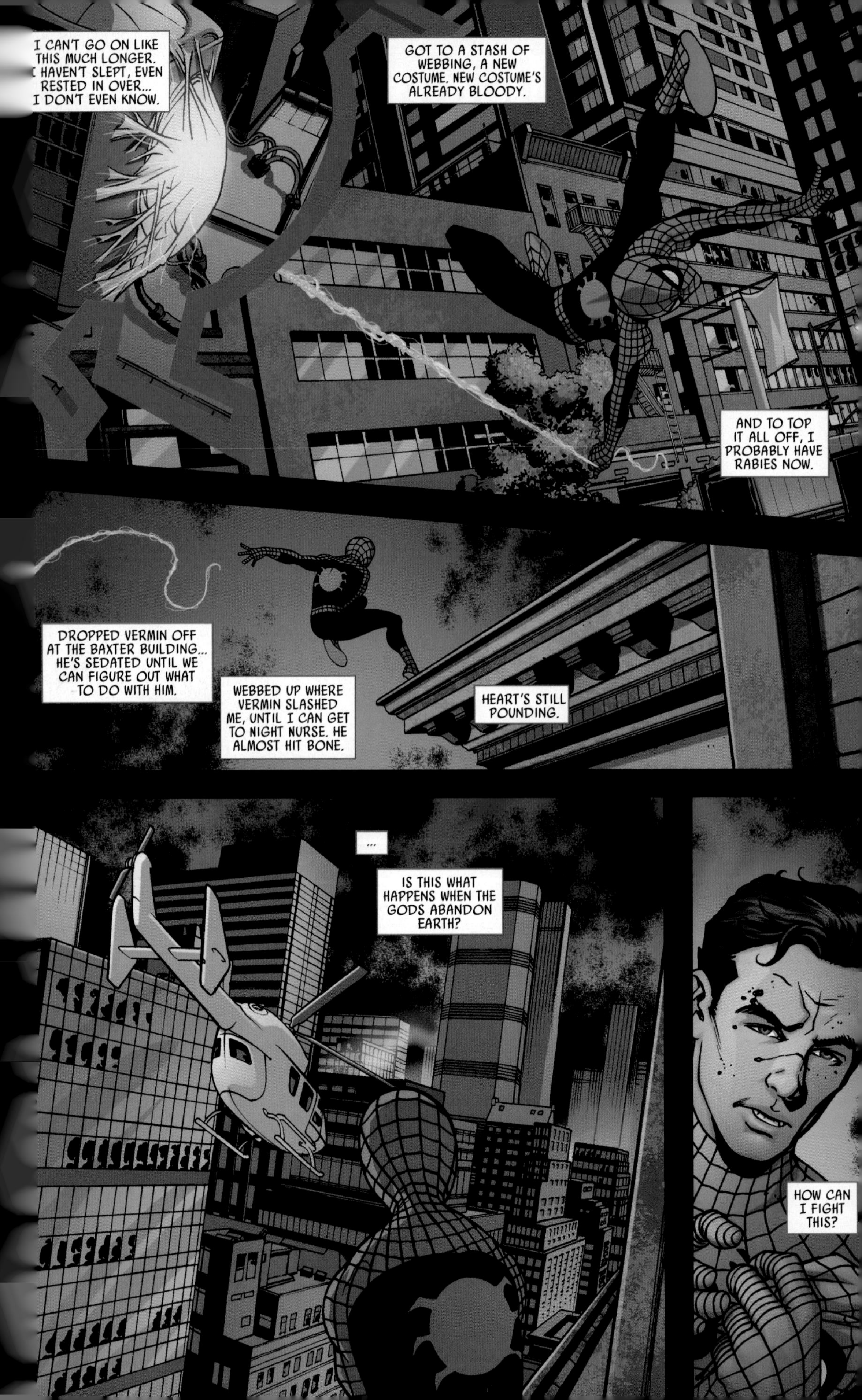
I CAN'T GO ON LIKE THIS MUCH LONGER. I HAVEN'T SLEPT, EVEN RESTED IN OVER... I DON'T EVEN KNOW.
GOT TO A STASH OF WEBBING, A NEW COSTUME. NEW COSTUME'S ALREADY BLOODY.
AND TO TOP IT ALL OFF, I PROBABLY HAVE RABIES NOW.
DROPPED VERMIN OFF AT THE BAXTER BUILDING... HE'S SEDATED UNTIL WE CAN FIGURE OUT WHAT TO DO WITH HIM.
WEBBED UP WHERE VERMIN SLASHED ME, UNTIL I CAN GET TO NIGHT NURSE. HE ALMOST HIT BONE.
HEART'S STILL POUNDING.
...
IS THIS WHAT HAPPENS WHEN THE GODS ABANDON EARTH?
HOW CAN I FIGHT THIS?

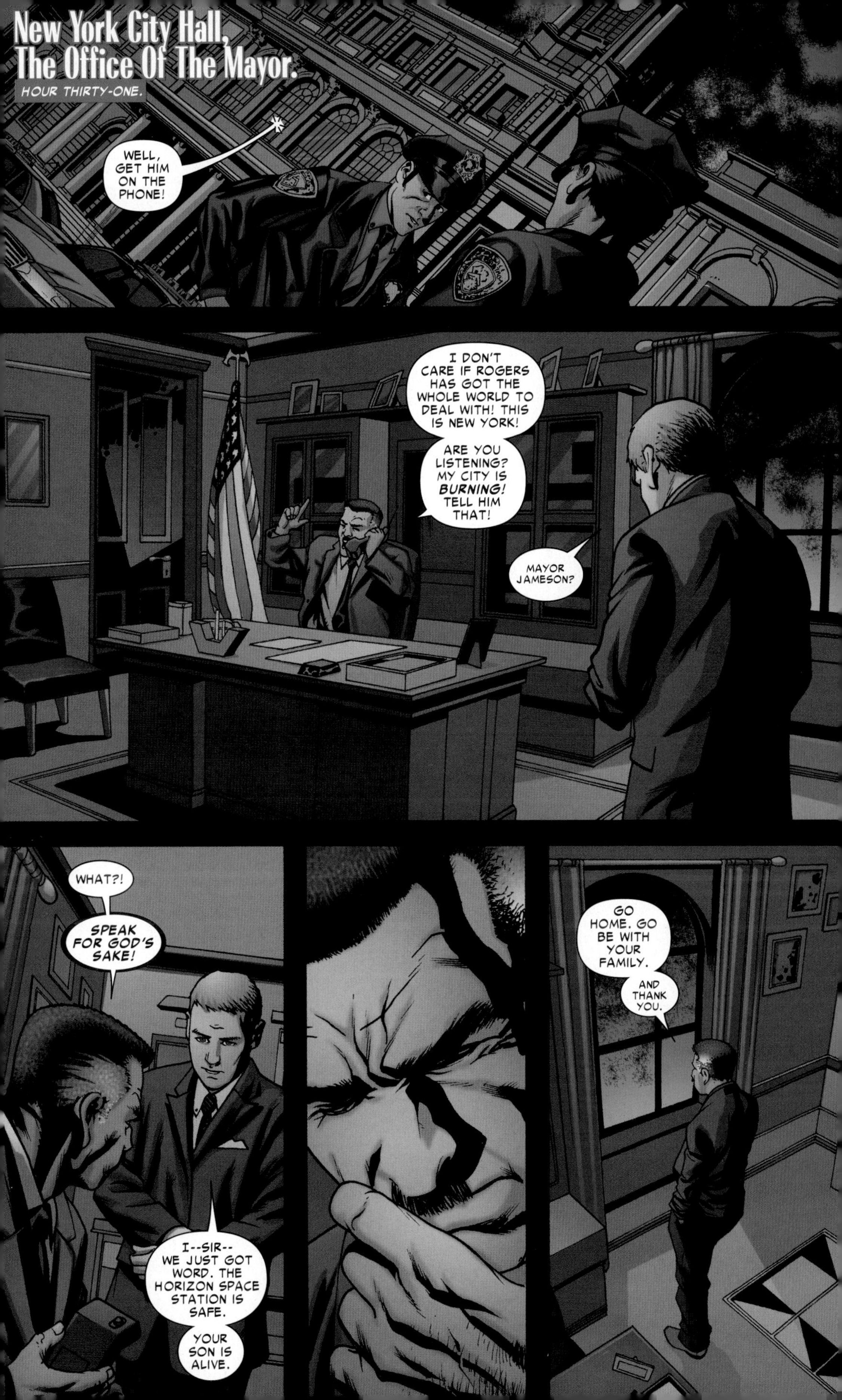
New York City Hall, The Office Of The Mayor.
HOUR THIRTY-ONE.
WELL, GET HIM ON THE PHONE!
I DON'T CARE IF ROGERS HAS GOT THE WHOLE WORLD TO DEAL WITH! THIS IS NEW YORK!
ARE YOU LISTENING? MY CITY IS BURNING! TELL HIM THAT!
MAYOR JAMESON?
WHAT?!
SPEAK FOR GOD'S SAKE!
I--SIR-- WE JUST GOT WORD. THE HORIZON SPACE STATION IS SAFE.
YOUR SON IS ALIVE.
GO HOME. GO BE WITH YOUR FAMILY.
AND THANK YOU.

Hour Thirty-Seven Of The Fear.

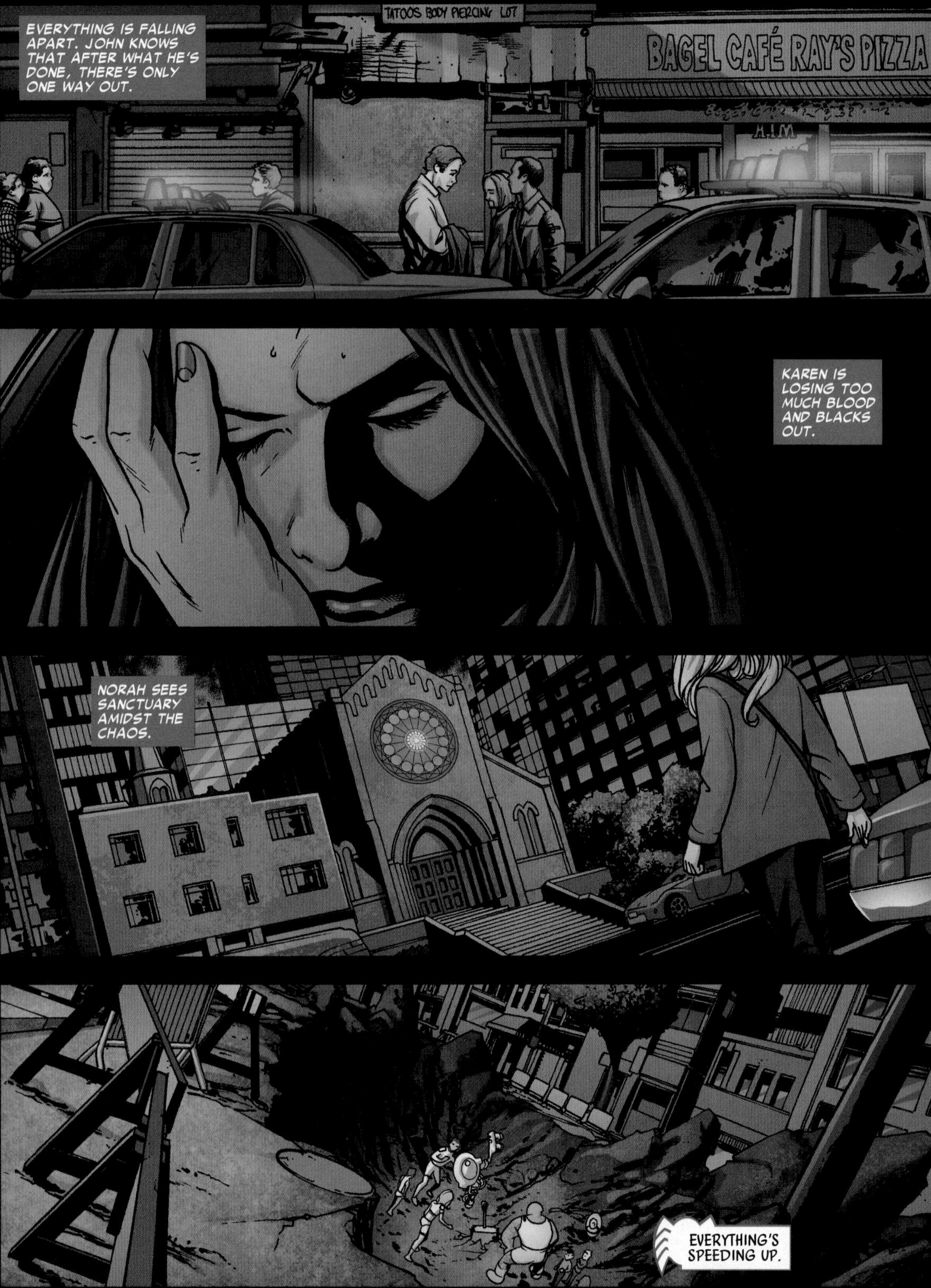

TATOOS BODY PIERCING LOT
BAGEL CAFÉ RAY'S PIZZA
EVERYTHING IS FALLING APART. JOHN KNOWS THAT AFTER WHAT HE'S DONE, THERE'S ONLY ONE WAY OUT.
KAREN IS LOSING TOO MUCH BLOOD AND BLACKS OUT.
NORAH SEES SANCTUARY AMIDST THE CHAOS.
EVERYTHING'S SPEEDING UP.

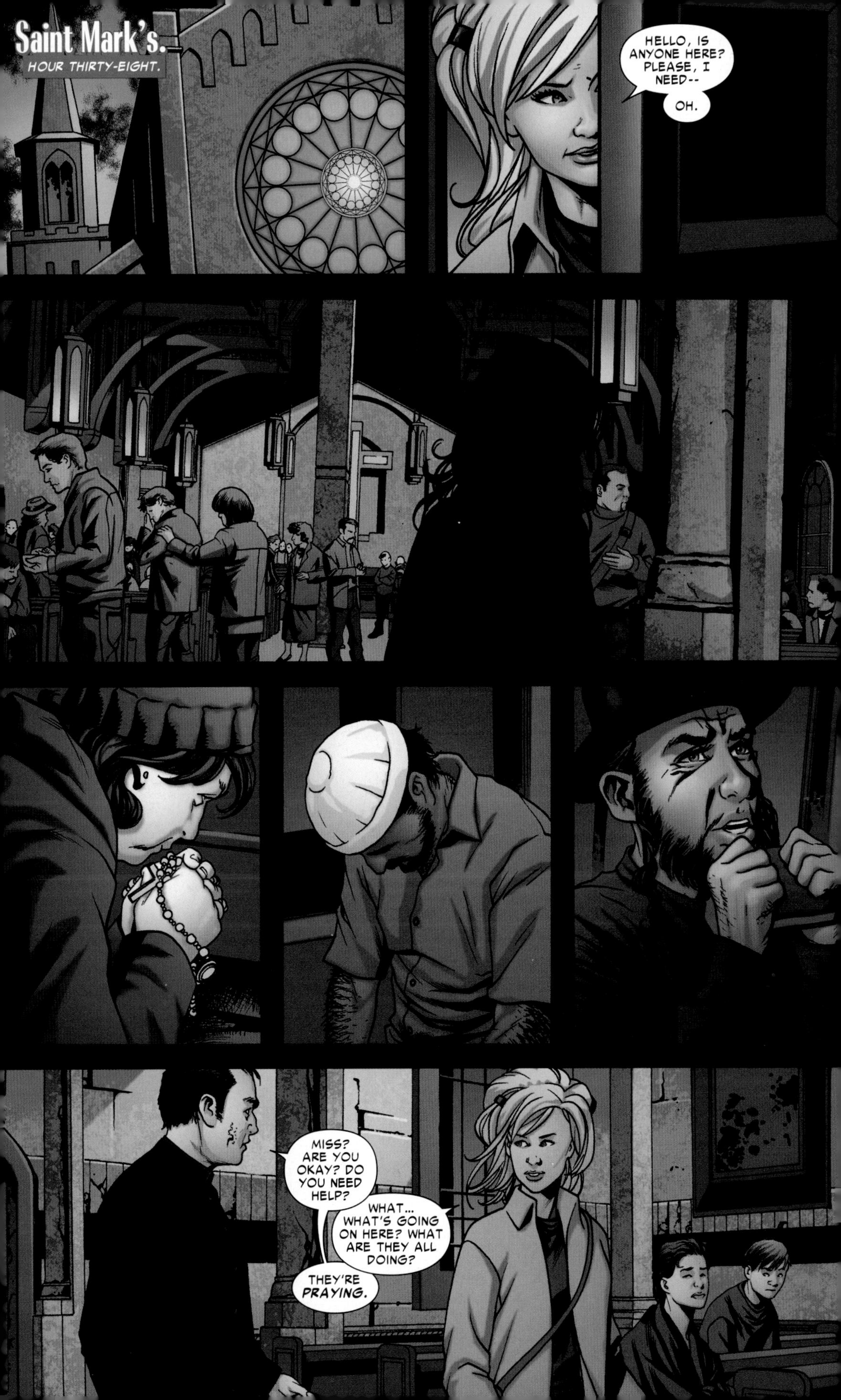
Saint Mark's.
HOUR THIRTY-EIGHT.
HELLO, IS ANYONE HERE? PLEASE, I NEED--
OH.
MISS? ARE YOU OKAY? DO YOU NEED HELP?
WHAT... WHAT'S GOING ON HERE? WHAT ARE THEY ALL DOING?
THEY'RE PRAYING.

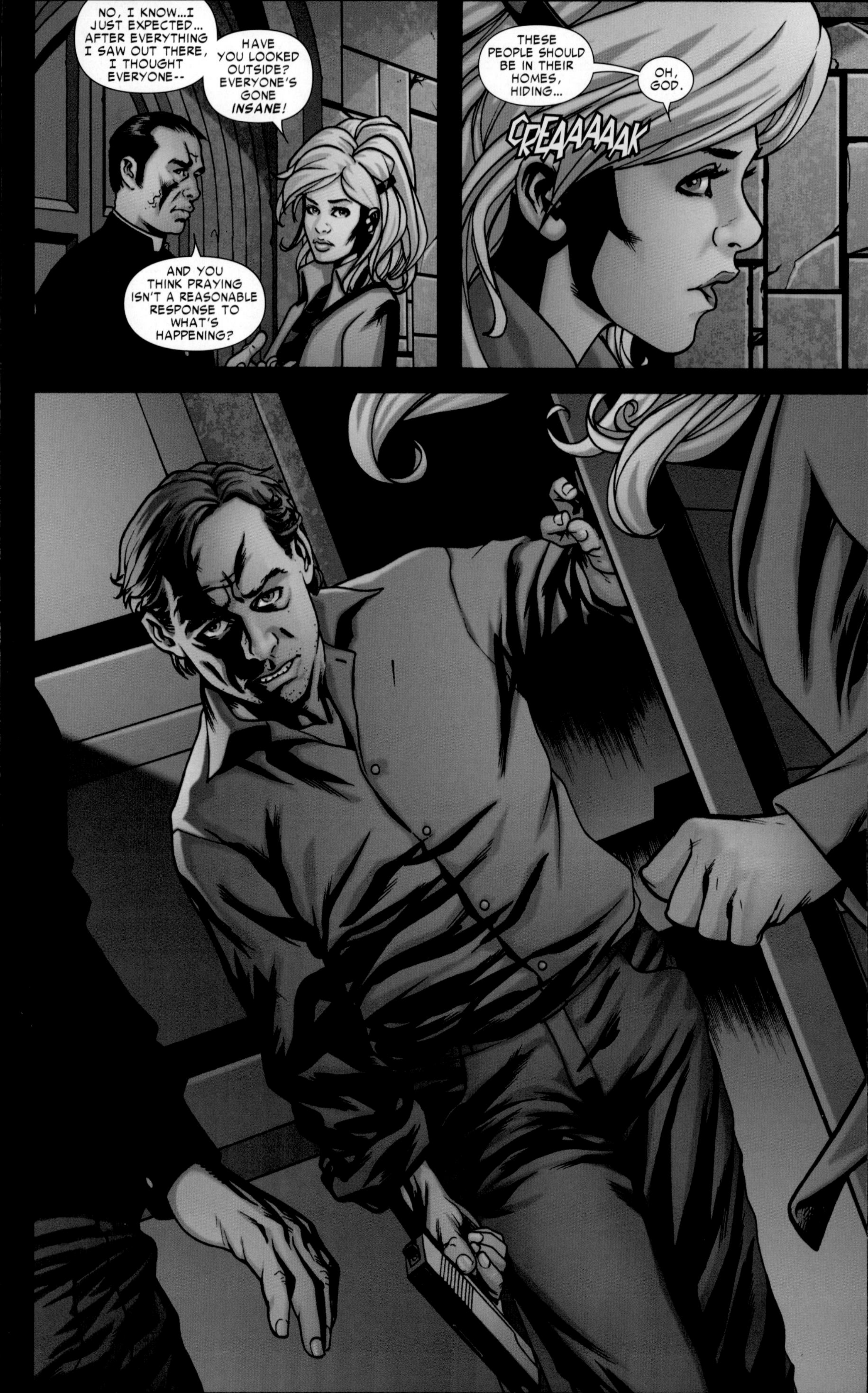
NO, I KNOW...I JUST EXPECTED... AFTER EVERYTHING I SAW OUT THERE, I THOUGHT EVERYONE--
HAVE YOU LOOKED OUTSIDE? EVERYONE'S GONE *INSANE!*
AND YOU THINK PRAYING ISN'T A REASONABLE RESPONSE TO WHAT'S HAPPENING?
THESE PEOPLE SHOULD BE IN THEIR HOMES, HIDING...
OH, GOD.
CREAAAAAK

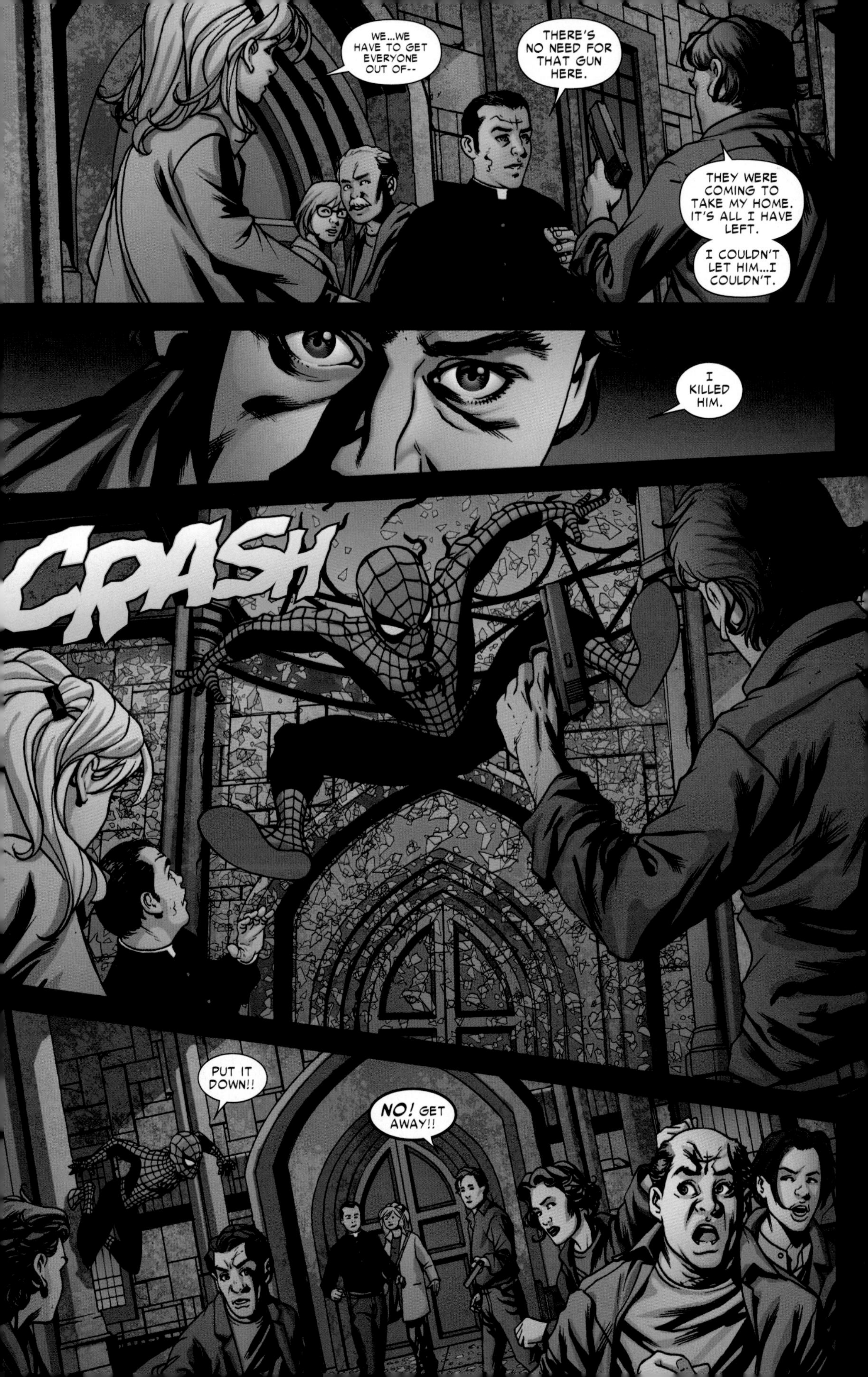
WE...WE HAVE TO GET EVERYONE OUT OF--
THERE'S NO NEED FOR THAT GUN HERE.
THEY WERE COMING TO TAKE MY HOME. IT'S ALL I HAVE LEFT.
I COULDN'T LET HIM...I COULDN'T.
I KILLED HIM.
CRASH
PUT IT DOWN!!
NO! GET AWAY!!

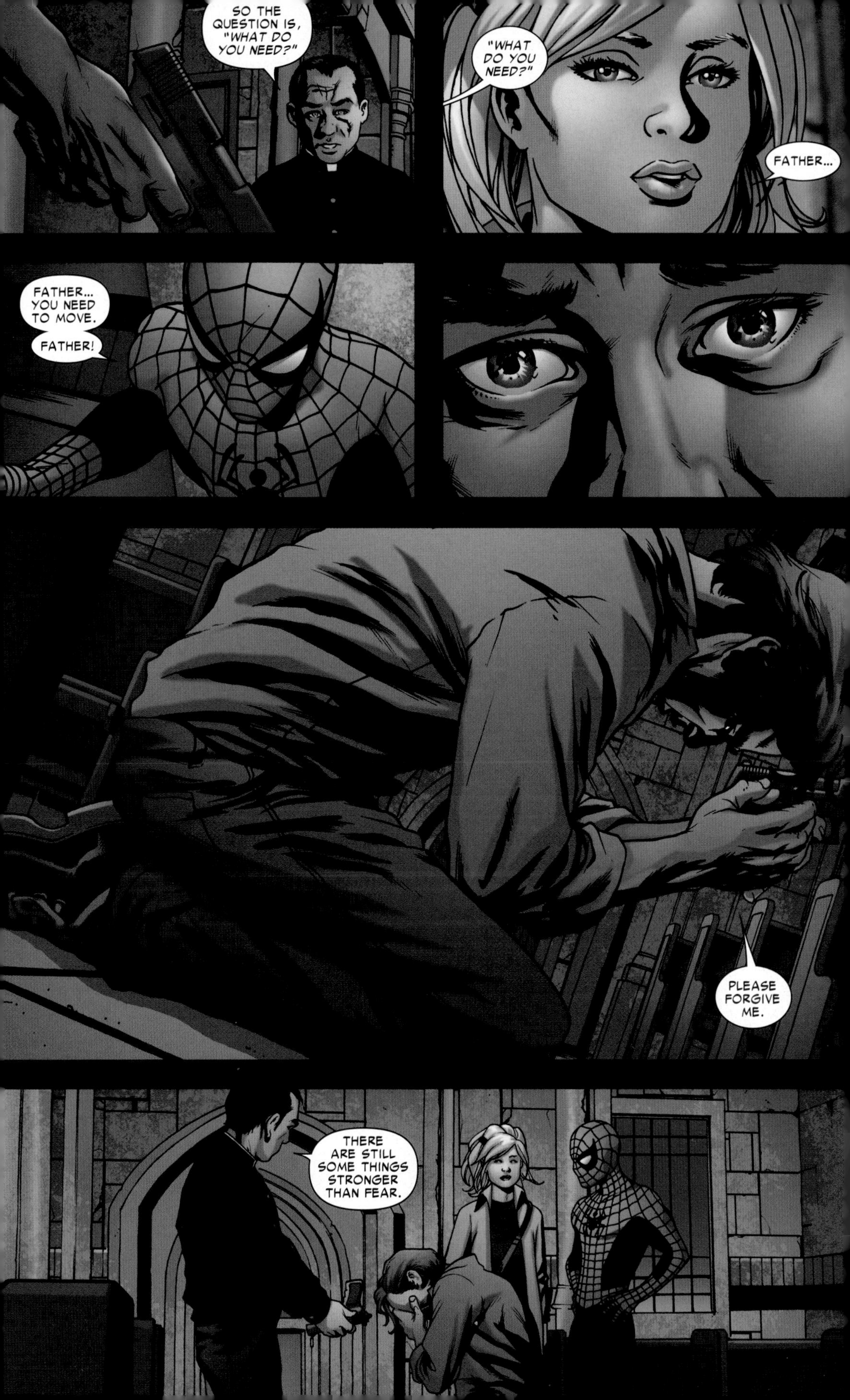
SO THE QUESTION IS, "WHAT DO YOU NEED?"
"WHAT DO YOU NEED?"
FATHER...
FATHER... YOU NEED TO MOVE.
FATHER!
PLEASE FORGIVE ME.
THERE ARE STILL SOME THINGS STRONGER THAN FEAR.

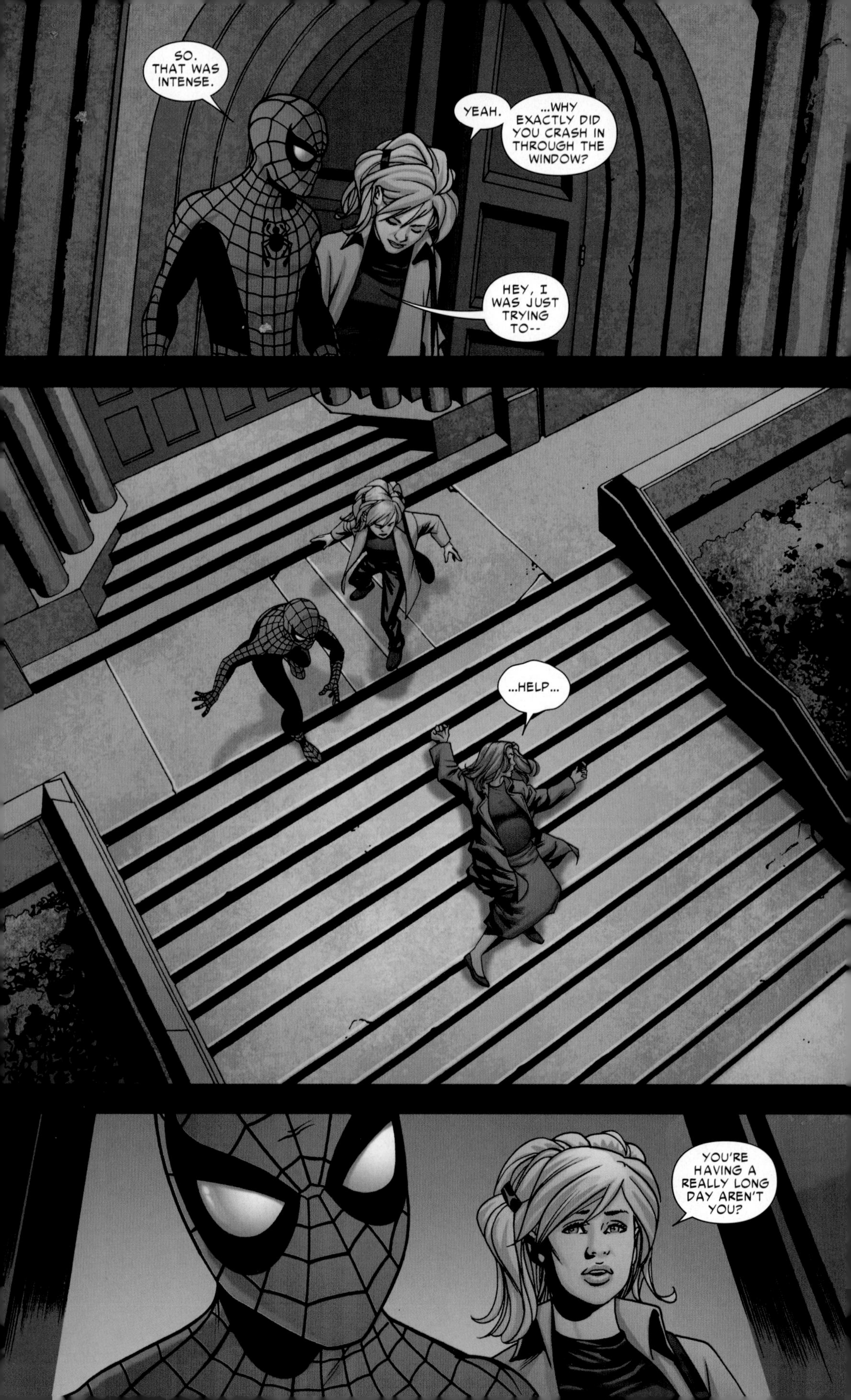
SO. THAT WAS INTENSE.
YEAH.
...WHY EXACTLY DID YOU CRASH IN THROUGH THE WINDOW?
HEY, I WAS JUST TRYING TO--
...HELP...
YOU'RE HAVING A REALLY LONG DAY AREN'T YOU?

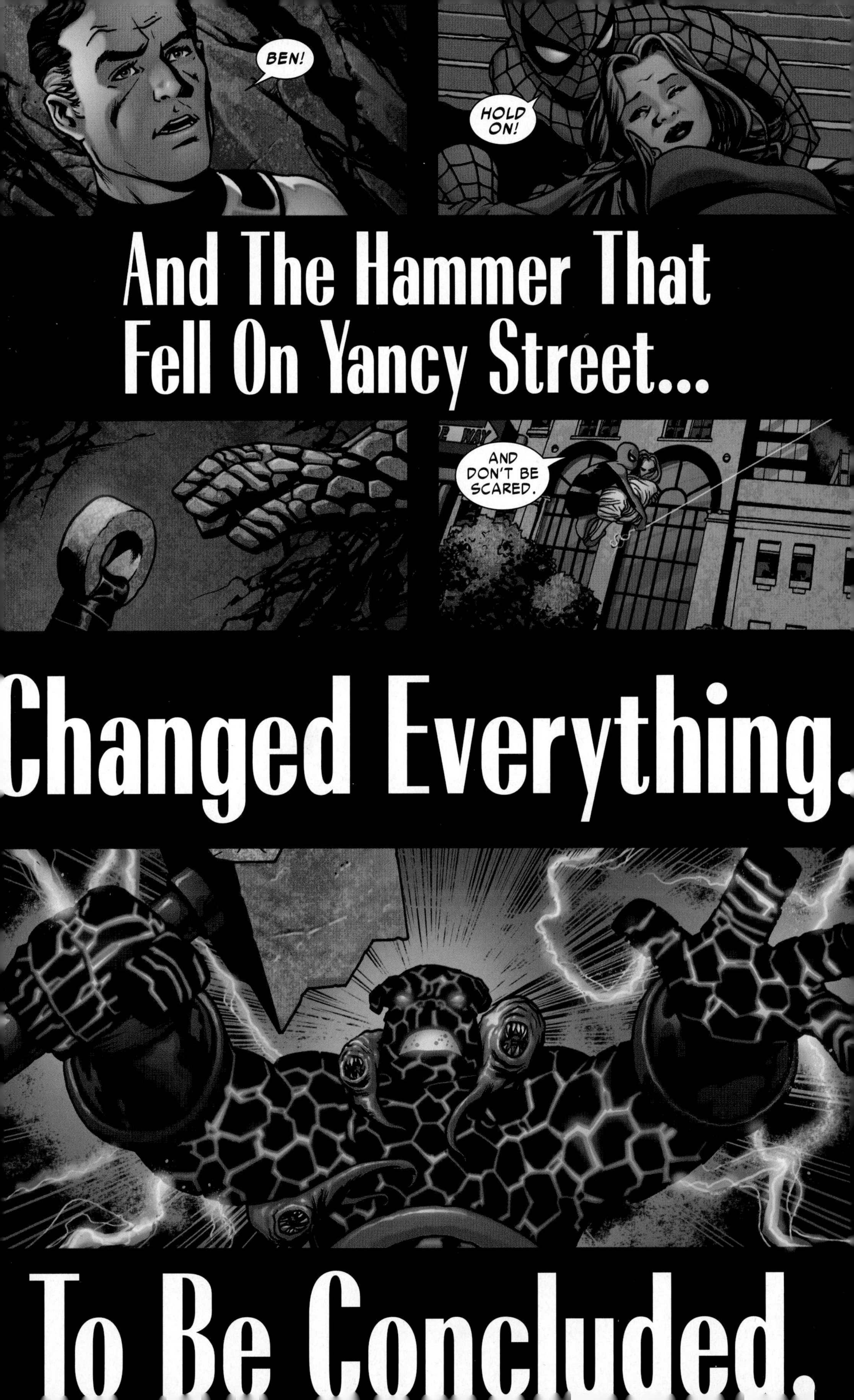
BEN!
HOLD ON!
And The Hammer That Fell On Yancy Street...
AND DON'T BE SCARED.
Changed Everything.
To Be Concluded.

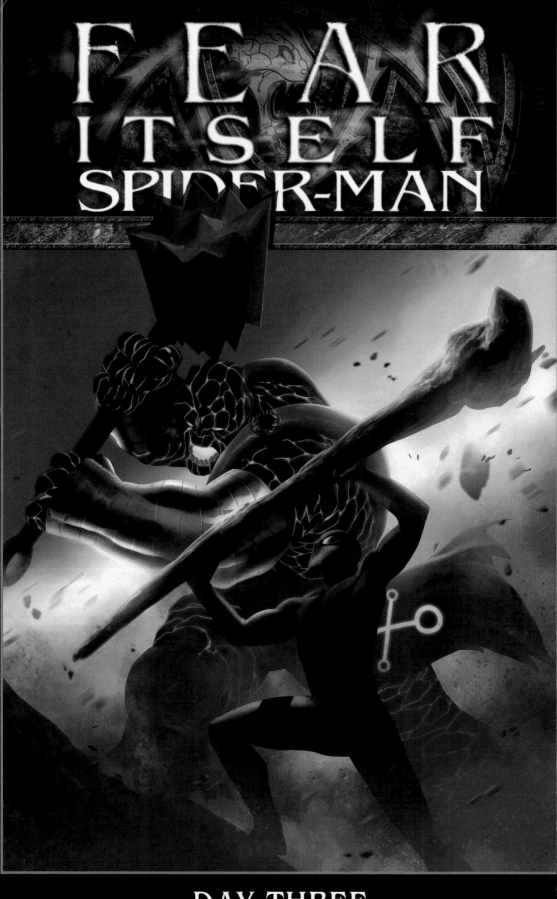

FEAR ITSELF
SPIDER-MAN

DAY THREE

Hour Forty-One Of The Fear

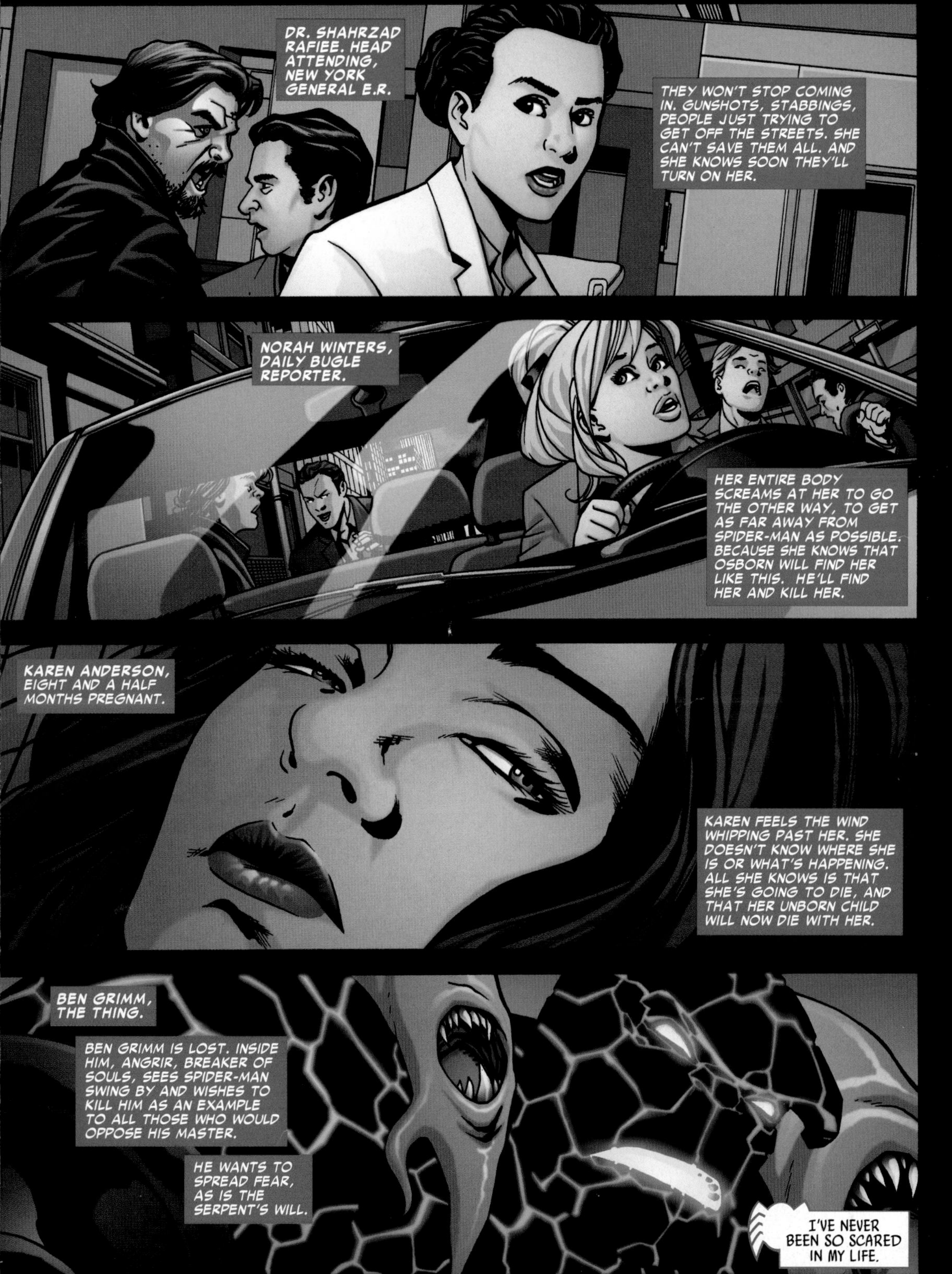

DR. SHAHRZAD RAFIEE. HEAD ATTENDING, NEW YORK GENERAL E.R.
THEY WON'T STOP COMING IN. GUNSHOTS, STABBINGS, PEOPLE JUST TRYING TO GET OFF THE STREETS. SHE CAN'T SAVE THEM ALL. AND SHE KNOWS SOON THEY'LL TURN ON HER.
NORAH WINTERS, DAILY BUGLE REPORTER.
HER ENTIRE BODY SCREAMS AT HER TO GO THE OTHER WAY, TO GET AS FAR AWAY FROM SPIDER-MAN AS POSSIBLE. BECAUSE SHE KNOWS THAT OSBORN WILL FIND HER LIKE THIS. HE'LL FIND HER AND KILL HER.
KAREN ANDERSON, EIGHT AND A HALF MONTHS PREGNANT.
KAREN FEELS THE WIND WHIPPING PAST HER. SHE DOESN'T KNOW WHERE SHE IS OR WHAT'S HAPPENING. ALL SHE KNOWS IS THAT SHE'S GOING TO DIE, AND THAT HER UNBORN CHILD WILL NOW DIE WITH HER.
BEN GRIMM, THE THING.
BEN GRIMM IS LOST. INSIDE HIM, ANGRIR, BREAKER OF SOULS, SEES SPIDER-MAN SWING BY AND WISHES TO KILL HIM AS AN EXAMPLE TO ALL THOSE WHO WOULD OPPOSE HIS MASTER.
HE WANTS TO SPREAD FEAR, AS IS THE SERPENT'S WILL.
I'VE NEVER BEEN SO SCARED IN MY LIFE.

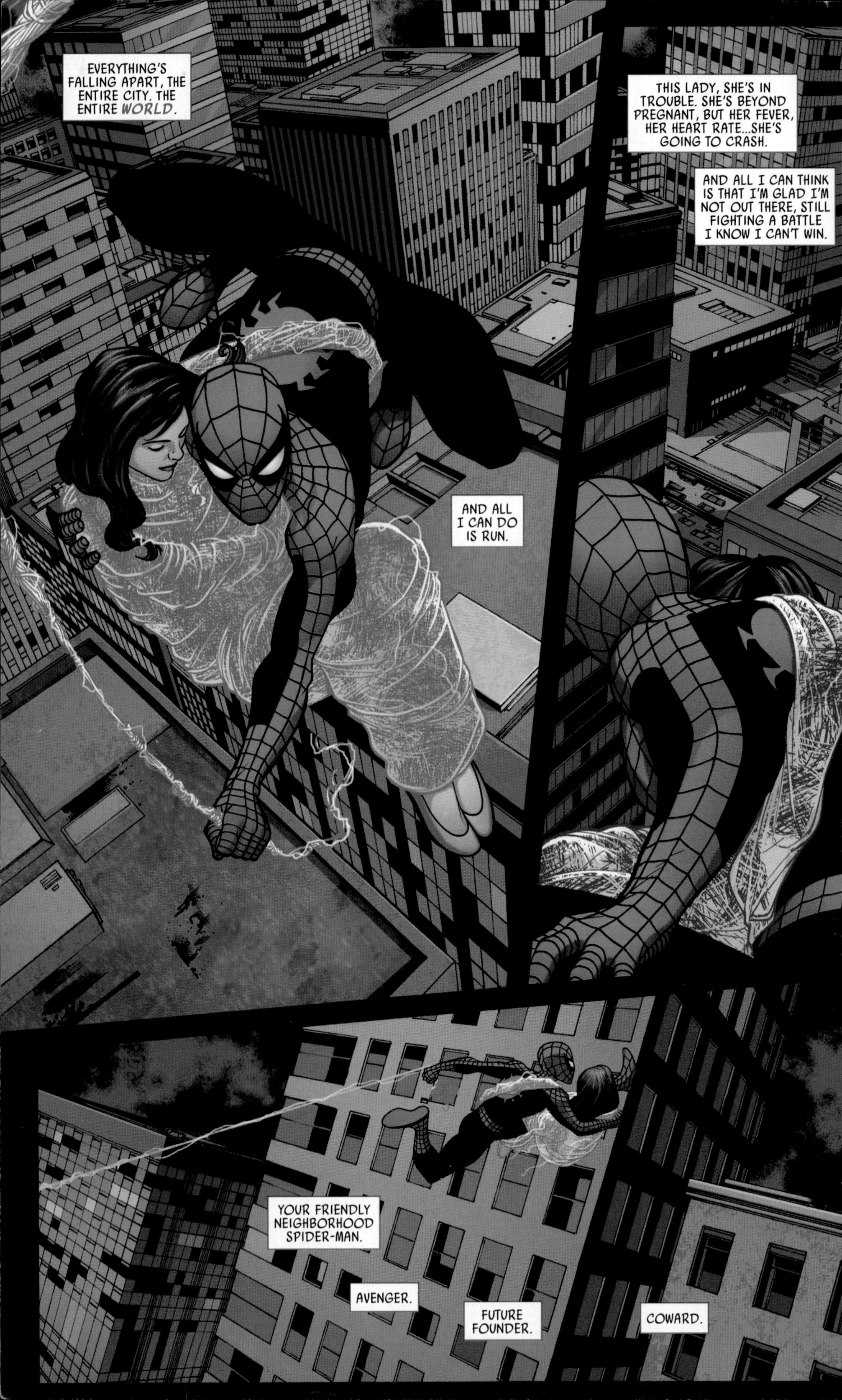
EVERYTHING'S FALLING APART, THE ENTIRE CITY. THE ENTIRE WORLD.
THIS LADY, SHE'S IN TROUBLE. SHE'S BEYOND PREGNANT, BUT HER FEVER, HER HEART RATE...SHE'S GOING TO CRASH.
AND ALL I CAN THINK IS THAT I'M GLAD I'M NOT OUT THERE, STILL FIGHTING A BATTLE I KNOW I CAN'T WIN.
AND ALL I CAN DO IS RUN.
YOUR FRIENDLY NEIGHBORHOOD SPIDER-MAN.
AVENGER.
FUTURE FOUNDER.
COWARD.

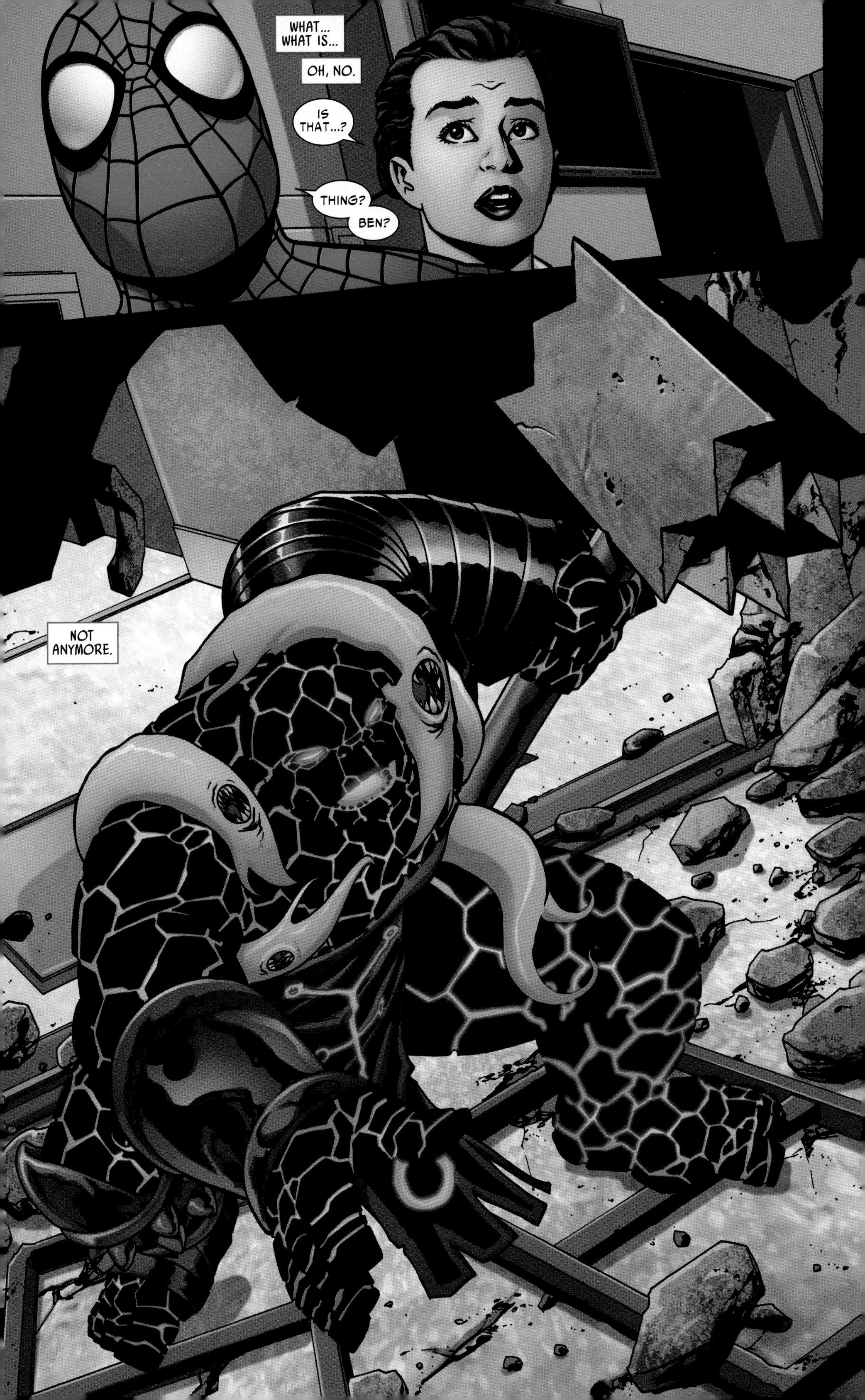
WHAT... WHAT IS...
OH, NO.
IS THAT...?
THING? BEN?
NOT ANYMORE.

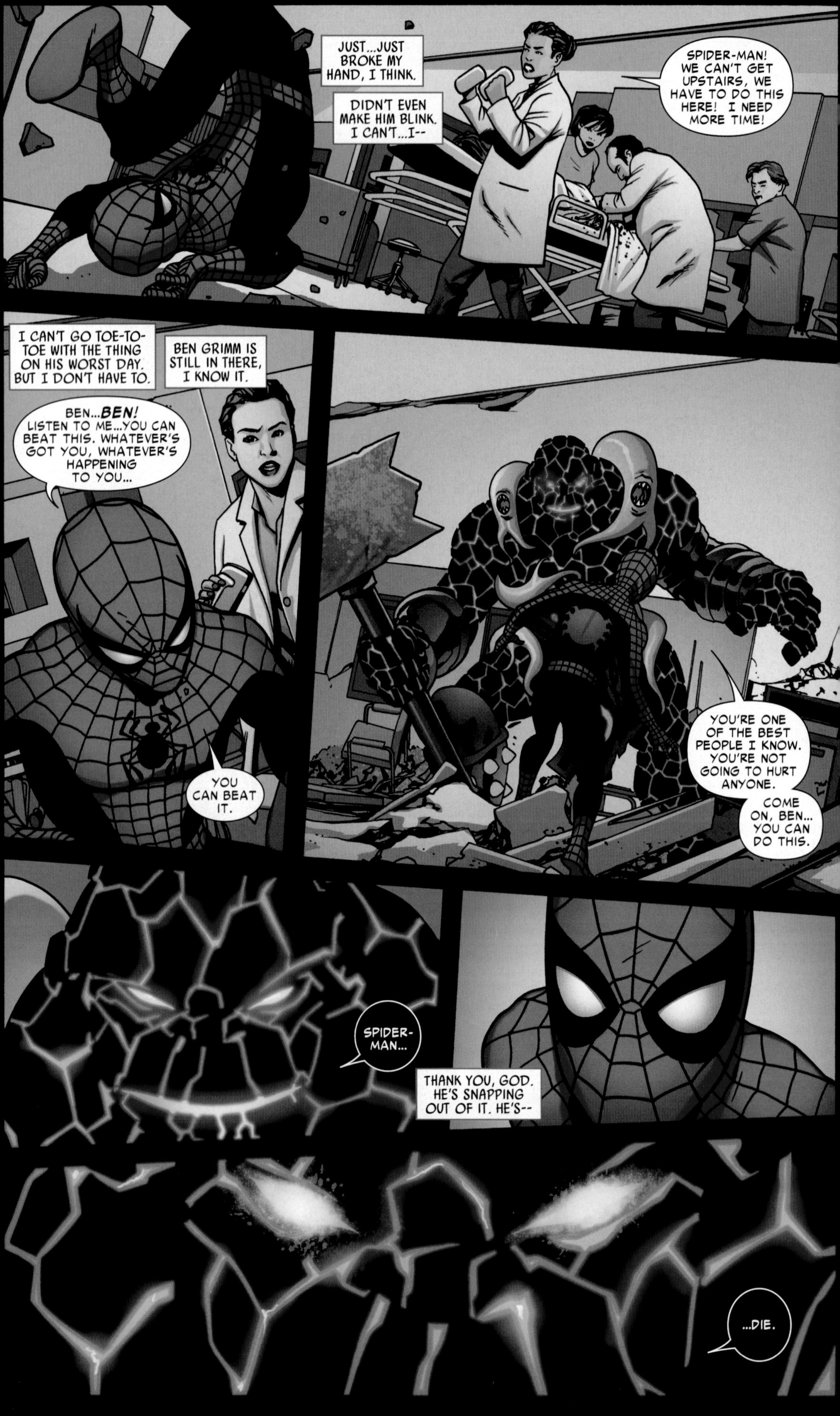
JUST...JUST BROKE MY HAND, I THINK.
DIDN'T EVEN MAKE HIM BLINK. I CAN'T...I--
SPIDER-MAN! WE CAN'T GET UPSTAIRS, WE HAVE TO DO THIS HERE! I NEED MORE TIME!
I CAN'T GO TOE-TO-TOE WITH THE THING ON HIS WORST DAY. BUT I DON'T HAVE TO.
BEN GRIMM IS STILL IN THERE, I KNOW IT.
BEN...BEN! LISTEN TO ME...YOU CAN BEAT THIS. WHATEVER'S GOT YOU, WHATEVER'S HAPPENING TO YOU...
YOU CAN BEAT IT.
YOU'RE ONE OF THE BEST PEOPLE I KNOW. YOU'RE NOT GOING TO HURT ANYONE.
COME ON, BEN... YOU CAN DO THIS.
SPIDER-MAN...
THANK YOU, GOD. HE'S SNAPPING OUT OF IT. HE'S--
...DIE.

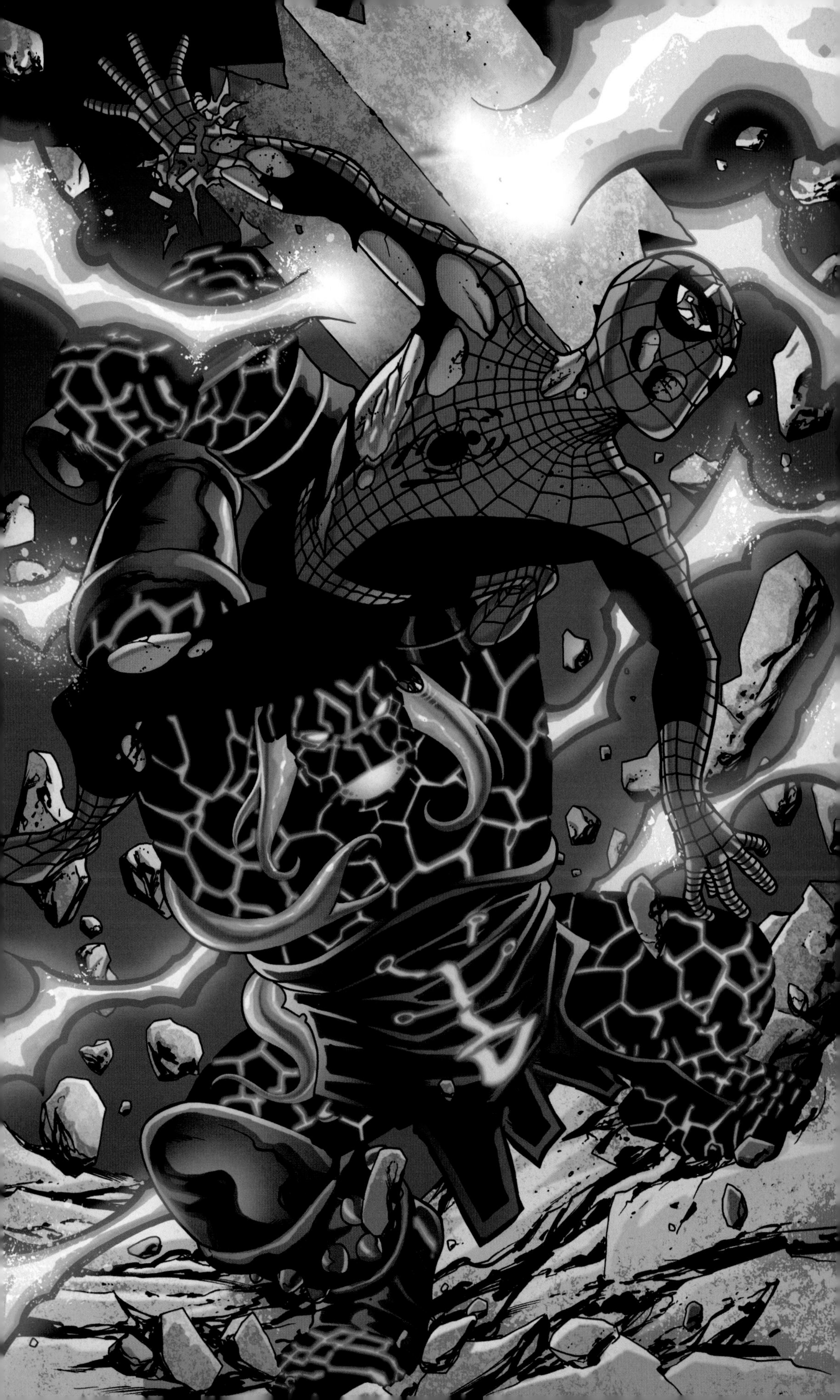

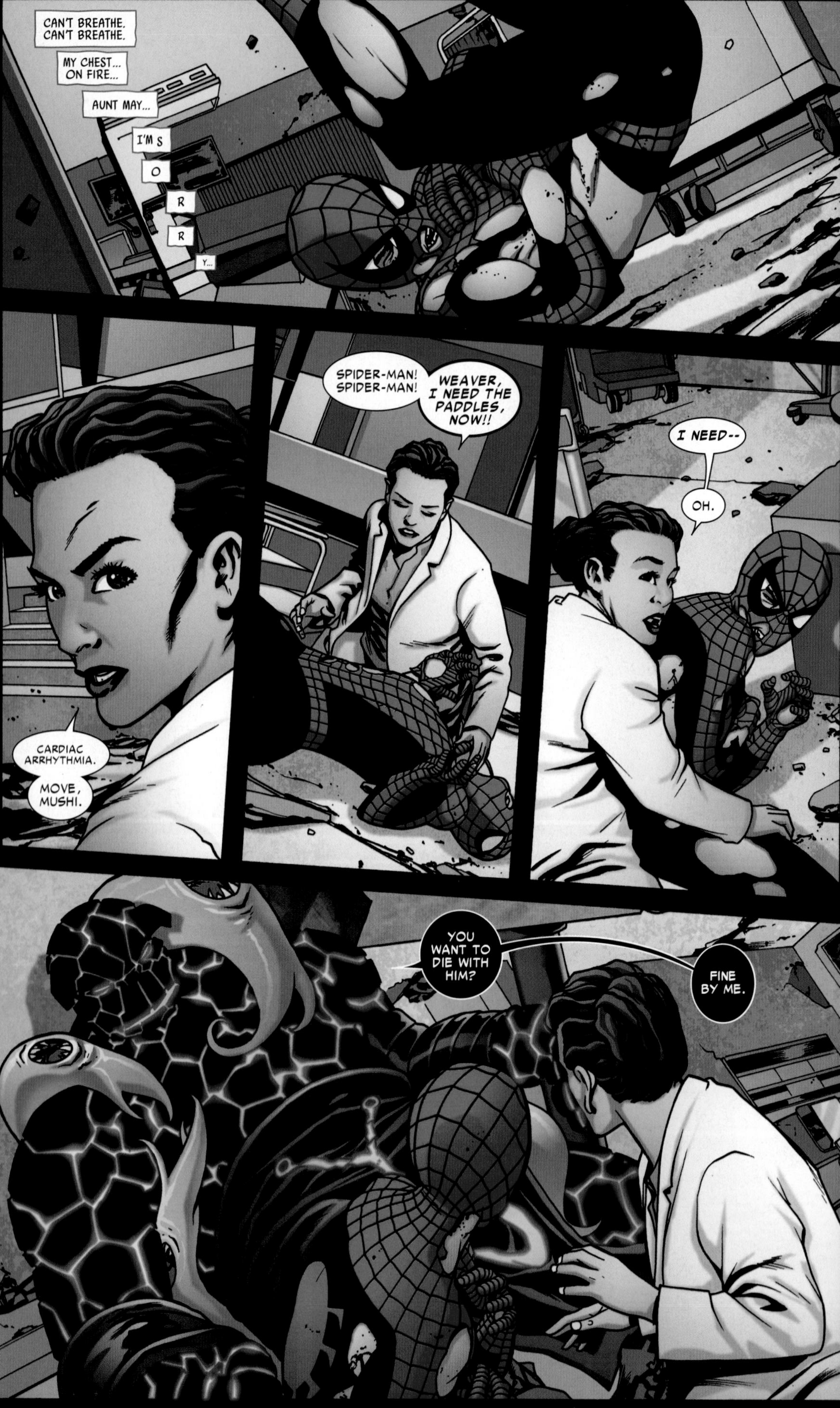
CAN'T BREATHE. CAN'T BREATHE.
MY CHEST... ON FIRE...
AUNT MAY...
I'M S
O
R
R
Y...
CARDIAC ARRHYTHMIA.
MOVE, MUSHI.
SPIDER-MAN! SPIDER-MAN!
WEAVER, I NEED THE PADDLES, NOW!!
I NEED--
OH.
YOU WANT TO DIE WITH HIM?
FINE BY ME.

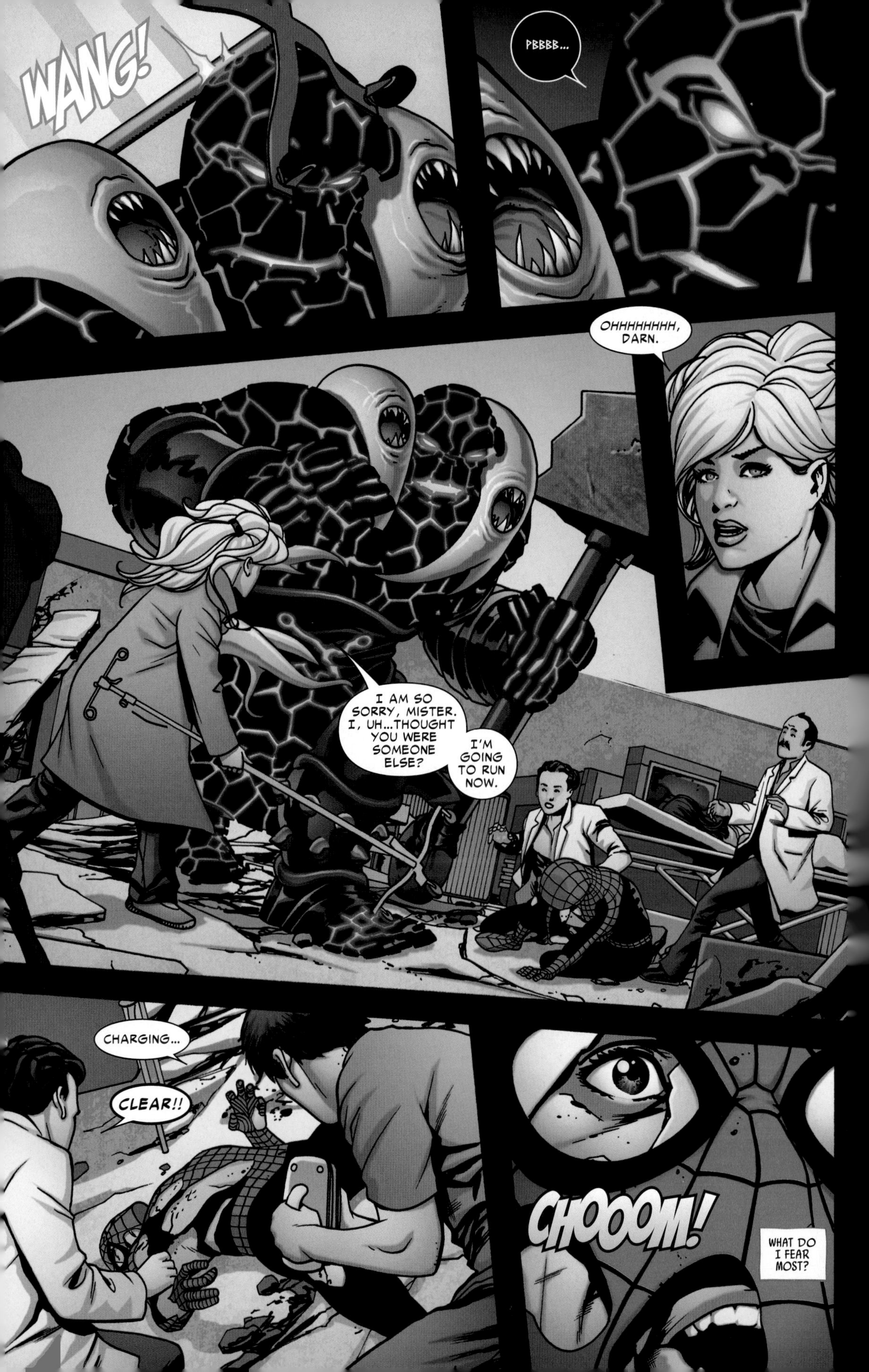
WANG!
PBBBB...
OHHHHHHHH, DARN.
I AM SO SORRY, MISTER. I, UH...THOUGHT YOU WERE SOMEONE ELSE?
I'M GOING TO RUN NOW.
CHARGING...
CLEAR!!
CHOOOM!
WHAT DO I FEAR MOST?

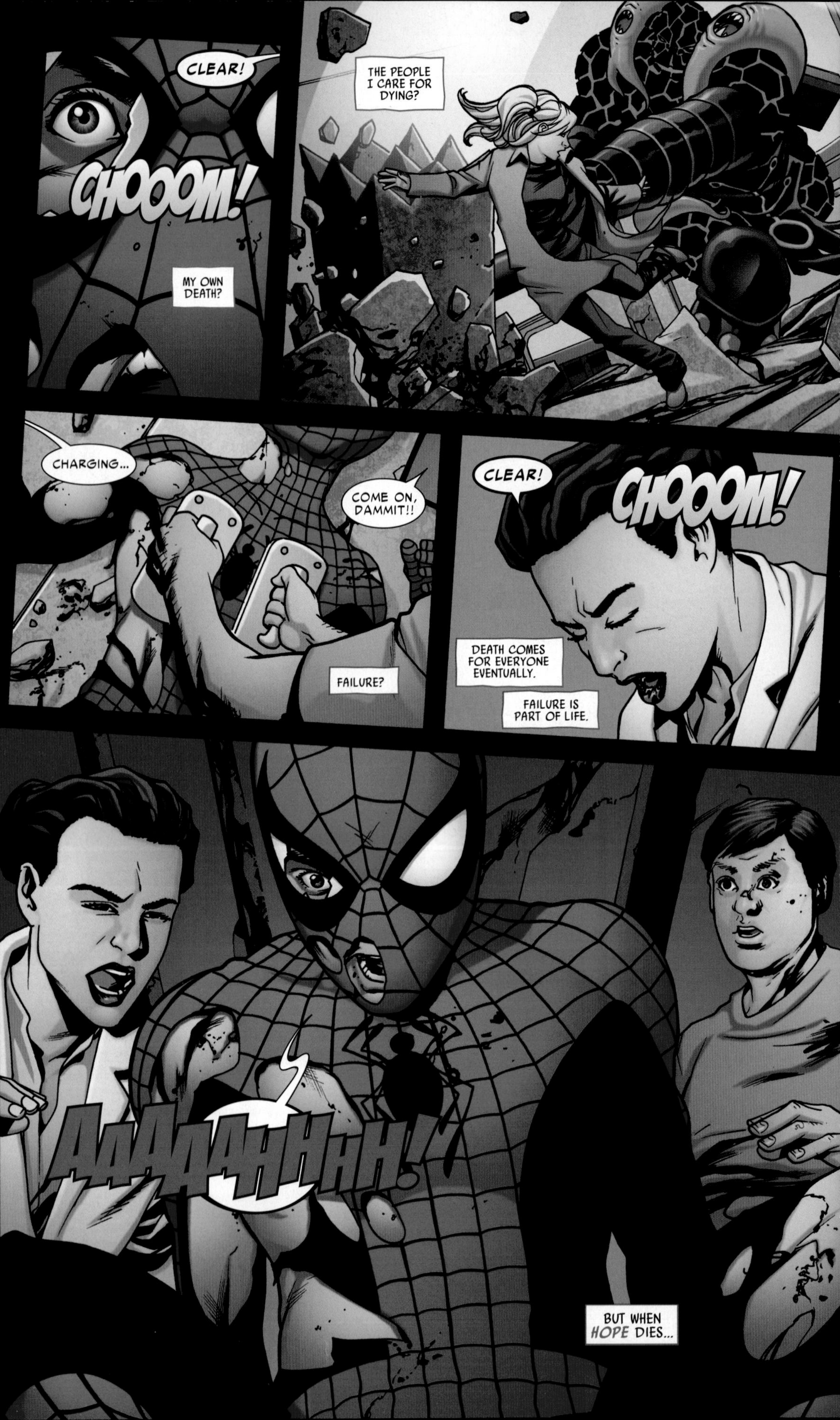
CLEAR!
CHOOOM!
MY OWN DEATH?
THE PEOPLE I CARE FOR DYING?
CHARGING...
COME ON, DAMMIT!!
FAILURE?
CLEAR!
CHOOOM!
DEATH COMES FOR EVERYONE EVENTUALLY.
FAILURE IS PART OF LIFE.
AAAAAHHHH!!
BUT WHEN HOPE DIES...

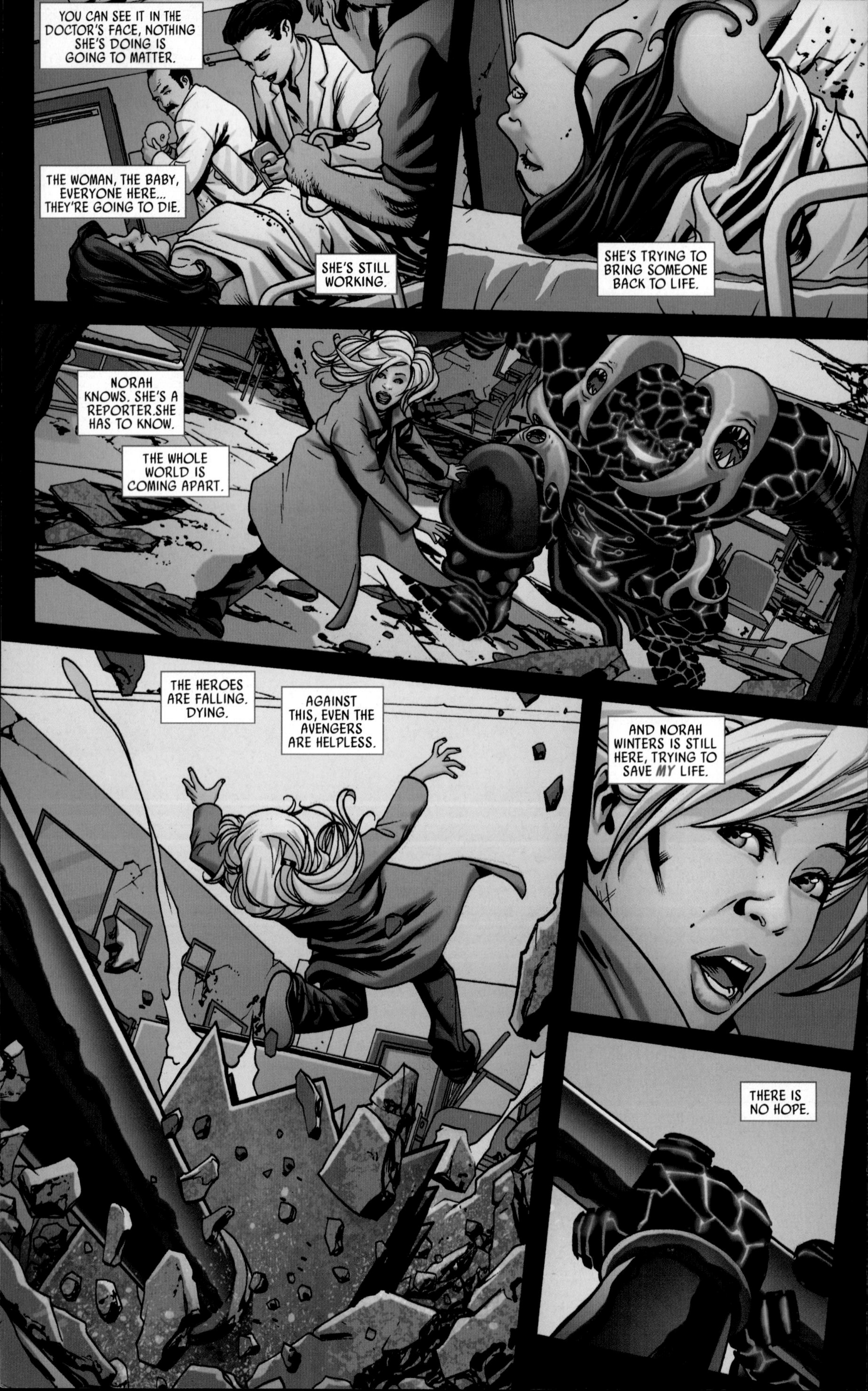
YOU CAN SEE IT IN THE DOCTOR'S FACE, NOTHING SHE'S DOING IS GOING TO MATTER.
THE WOMAN, THE BABY, EVERYONE HERE... THEY'RE GOING TO DIE.
SHE'S STILL WORKING.
SHE'S TRYING TO BRING SOMEONE BACK TO LIFE.
NORAH KNOWS. SHE'S A REPORTER.SHE HAS TO KNOW.
THE WHOLE WORLD IS COMING APART.
THE HEROES ARE FALLING. DYING.
AGAINST THIS, EVEN THE AVENGERS ARE HELPLESS.
AND NORAH WINTERS IS STILL HERE, TRYING TO SAVE MY LIFE.
THERE IS NO HOPE.

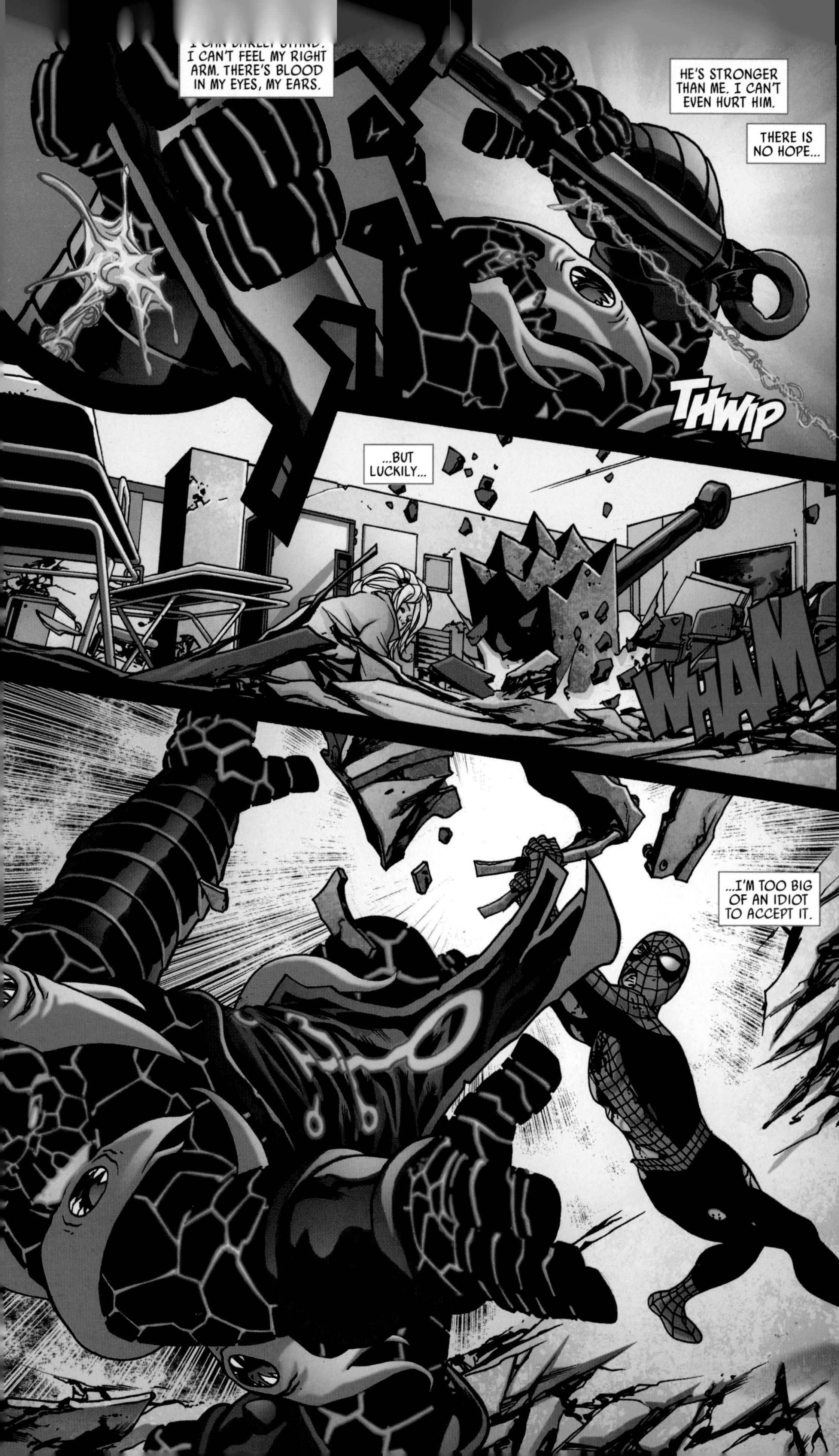
I CAN'T FEEL MY RIGHT ARM. THERE'S BLOOD IN MY EYES, MY EARS.
HE'S STRONGER THAN ME. I CAN'T EVEN HURT HIM.
THERE IS NO HOPE...
THWIP
...BUT LUCKILY...
WHAM
...I'M TOO BIG OF AN IDIOT TO ACCEPT IT.

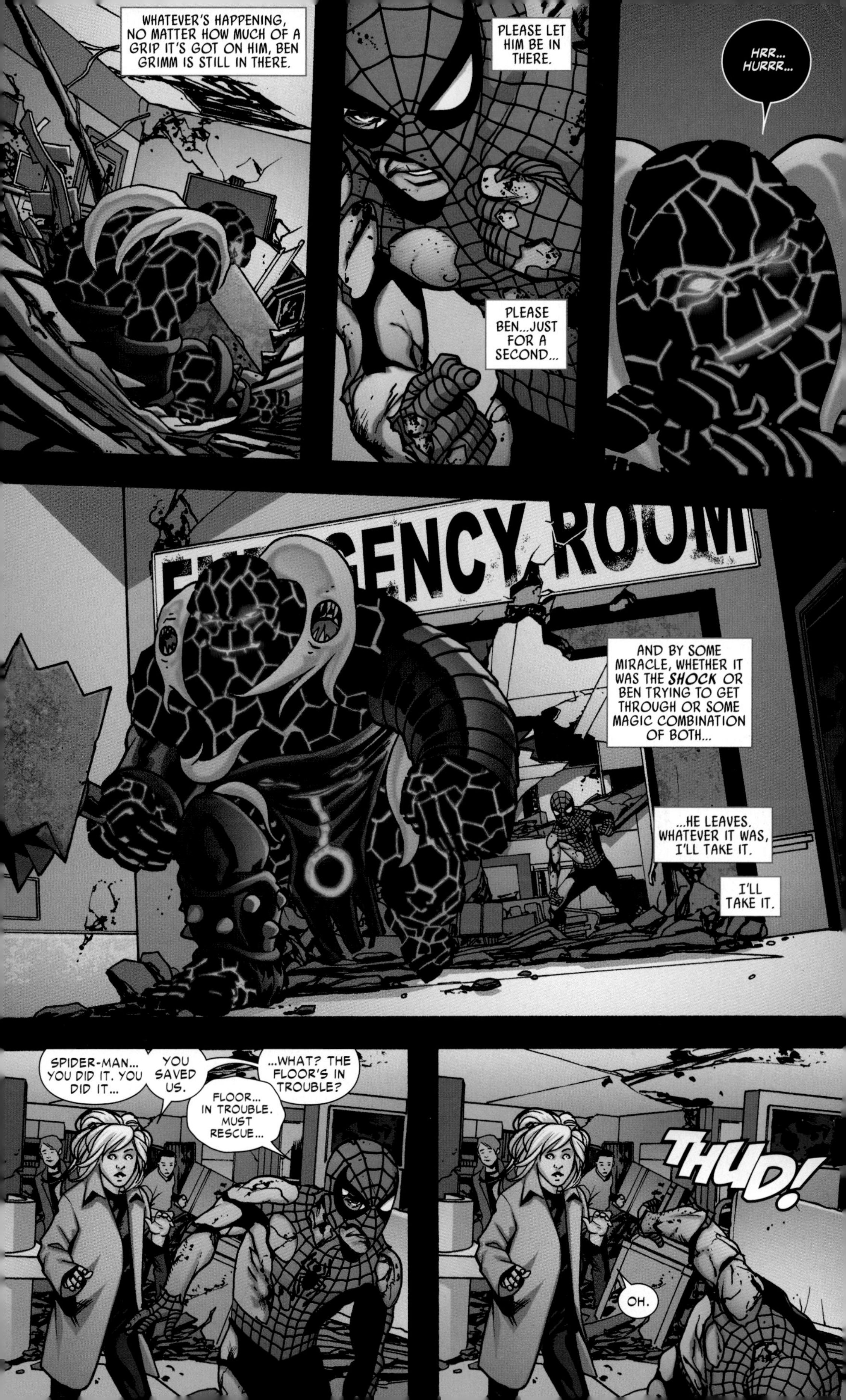
WHATEVER'S HAPPENING, NO MATTER HOW MUCH OF A GRIP IT'S GOT ON HIM, BEN GRIMM IS STILL IN THERE.
PLEASE LET HIM BE IN THERE.
PLEASE BEN...JUST FOR A SECOND...
HRR... HURRR...
EMERGENCY ROOM
AND BY SOME MIRACLE, WHETHER IT WAS THE SHOCK OR BEN TRYING TO GET THROUGH OR SOME MAGIC COMBINATION OF BOTH...
...HE LEAVES. WHATEVER IT WAS, I'LL TAKE IT.
I'LL TAKE IT.
SPIDER-MAN... YOU DID IT. YOU DID IT...
YOU SAVED US.
FLOOR... IN TROUBLE. MUST RESCUE...
...WHAT? THE FLOOR'S IN TROUBLE?
THUD!
OH.

Hour Forty-Eight Of The Fear

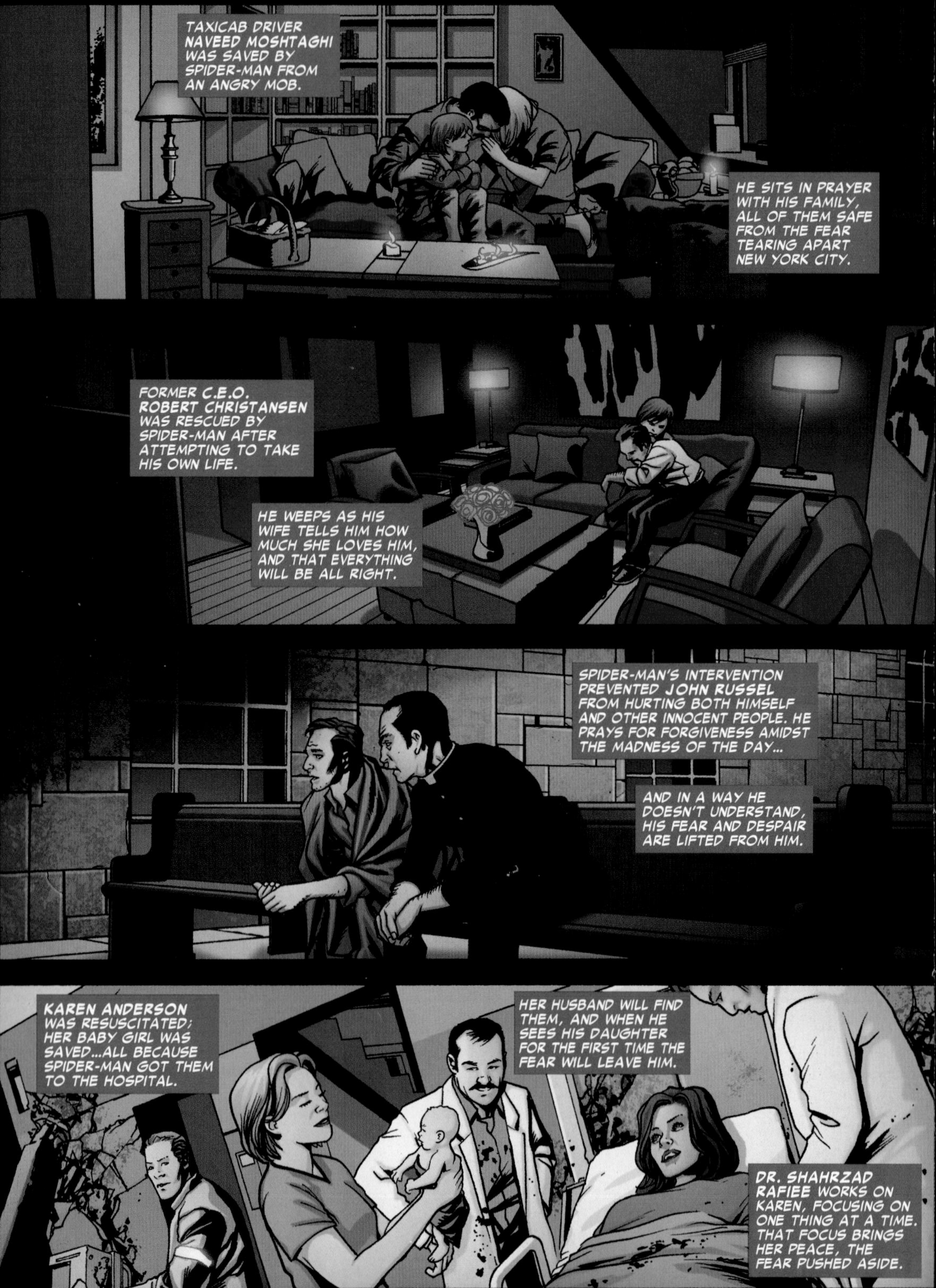
TAXICAB DRIVER NAVEED MOSHTAGHI WAS SAVED BY SPIDER-MAN FROM AN ANGRY MOB.
HE SITS IN PRAYER WITH HIS FAMILY, ALL OF THEM SAFE FROM THE FEAR TEARING APART NEW YORK CITY.
FORMER C.E.O. ROBERT CHRISTANSEN WAS RESCUED BY SPIDER-MAN AFTER ATTEMPTING TO TAKE HIS OWN LIFE.
HE WEEPS AS HIS WIFE TELLS HIM HOW MUCH SHE LOVES HIM, AND THAT EVERYTHING WILL BE ALL RIGHT.
SPIDER-MAN'S INTERVENTION PREVENTED JOHN RUSSEL FROM HURTING BOTH HIMSELF AND OTHER INNOCENT PEOPLE. HE PRAYS FOR FORGIVENESS AMIDST THE MADNESS OF THE DAY...
AND IN A WAY HE DOESN'T UNDERSTAND, HIS FEAR AND DESPAIR ARE LIFTED FROM HIM.
KAREN ANDERSON WAS RESUSCITATED; HER BABY GIRL WAS SAVED...ALL BECAUSE SPIDER-MAN GOT THEM TO THE HOSPITAL.
HER HUSBAND WILL FIND THEM, AND WHEN HE SEES HIS DAUGHTER FOR THE FIRST TIME THE FEAR WILL LEAVE HIM.
DR. SHAHRZAD RAFIEE WORKS ON KAREN, FOCUSING ON ONE THING AT A TIME. THAT FOCUS BRINGS HER PEACE, THE FEAR PUSHED ASIDE.

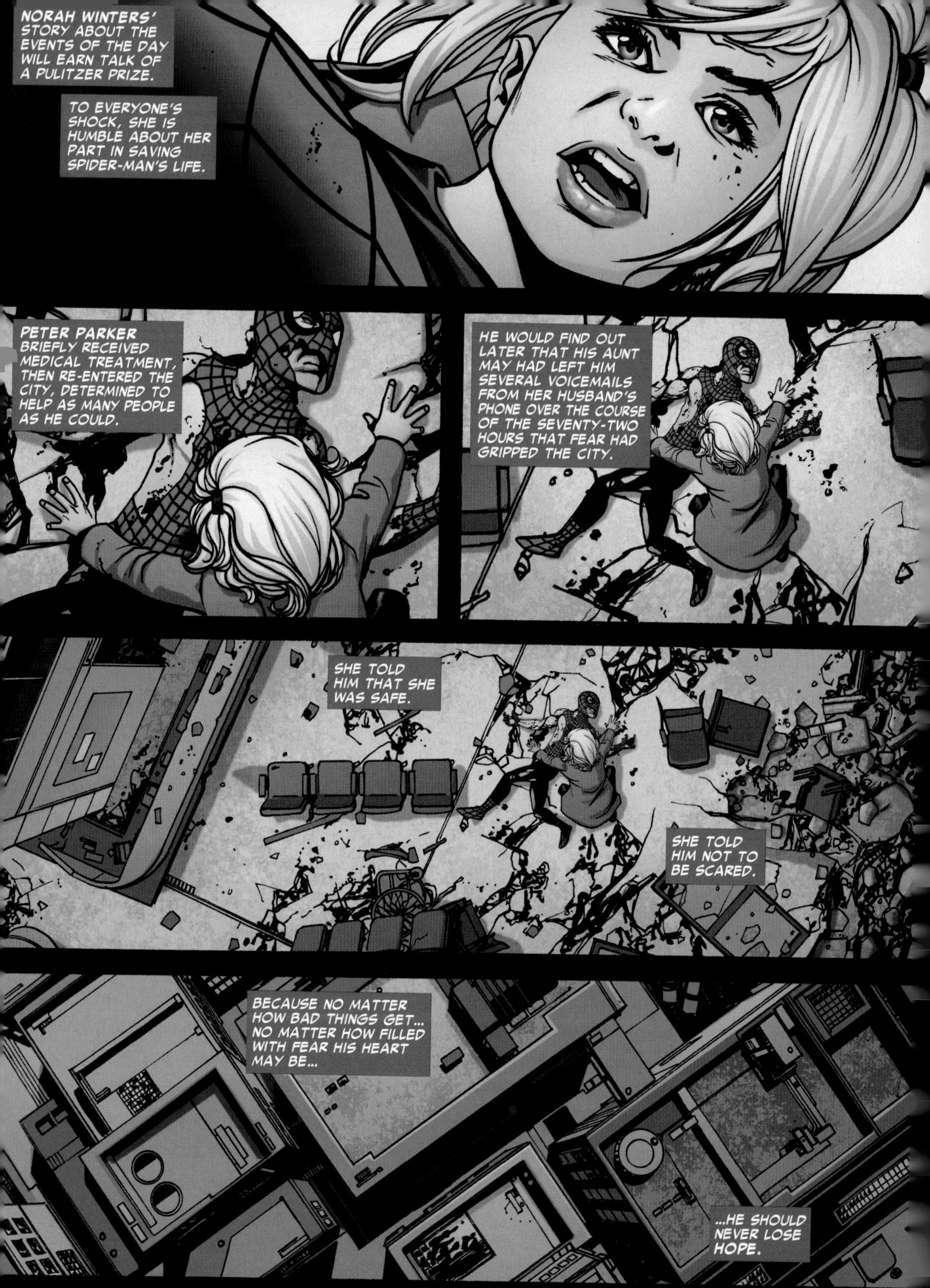
NORAH WINTERS' STORY ABOUT THE EVENTS OF THE DAY WILL EARN TALK OF A PULITZER PRIZE.
TO EVERYONE'S SHOCK, SHE IS HUMBLE ABOUT HER PART IN SAVING SPIDER-MAN'S LIFE.
PETER PARKER BRIEFLY RECEIVED MEDICAL TREATMENT, THEN RE-ENTERED THE CITY, DETERMINED TO HELP AS MANY PEOPLE AS HE COULD.
HE WOULD FIND OUT LATER THAT HIS AUNT MAY HAD LEFT HIM SEVERAL VOICEMAILS FROM HER HUSBAND'S PHONE OVER THE COURSE OF THE SEVENTY-TWO HOURS THAT FEAR HAD GRIPPED THE CITY.
SHE TOLD HIM THAT SHE WAS SAFE.
SHE TOLD HIM NOT TO BE SCARED.
BECAUSE NO MATTER HOW BAD THINGS GET... NO MATTER HOW FILLED WITH FEAR HIS HEART MAY BE...
...HE SHOULD NEVER LOSE HOPE.

The End

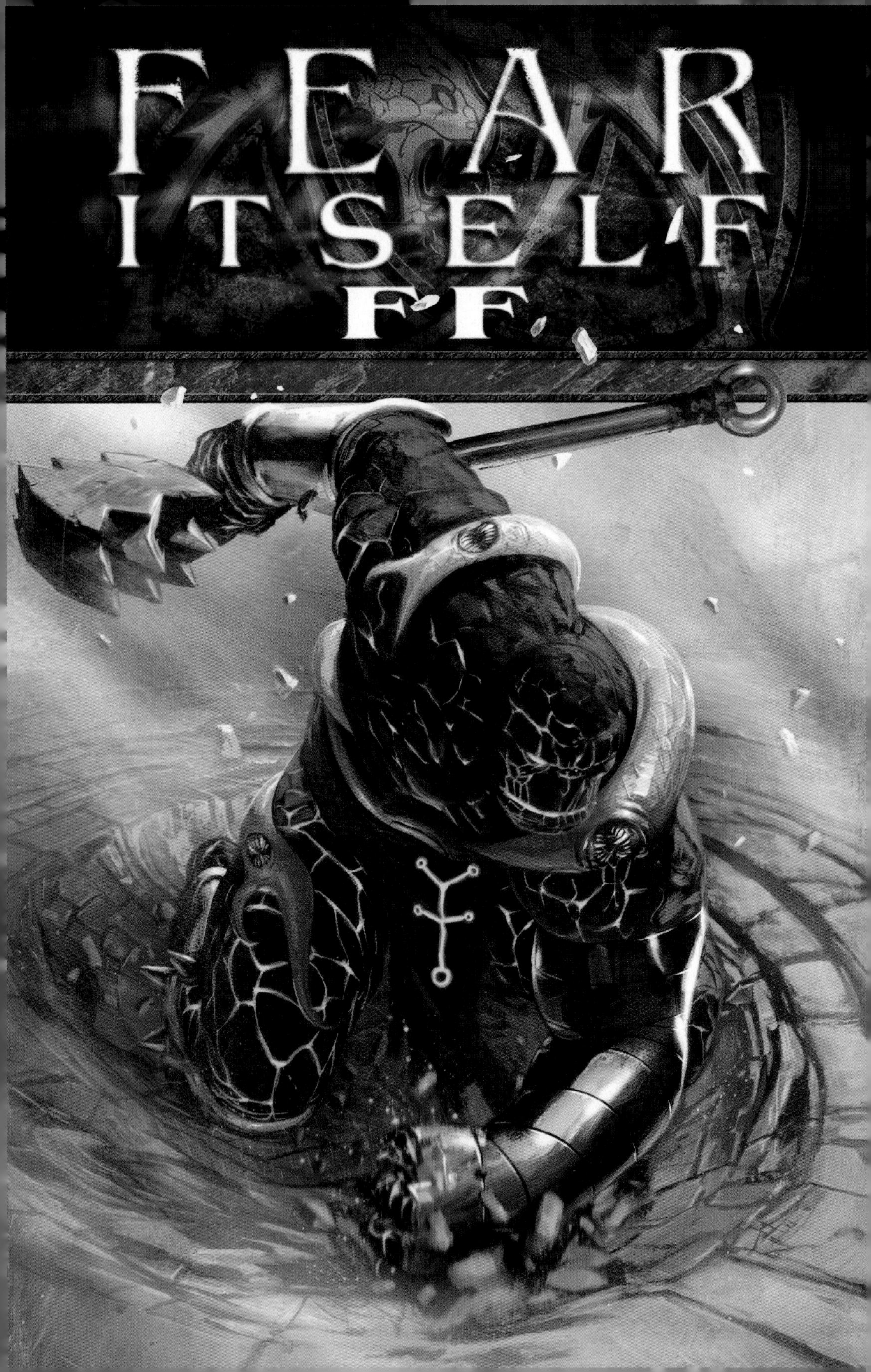
FEAR
ITSELF
FF

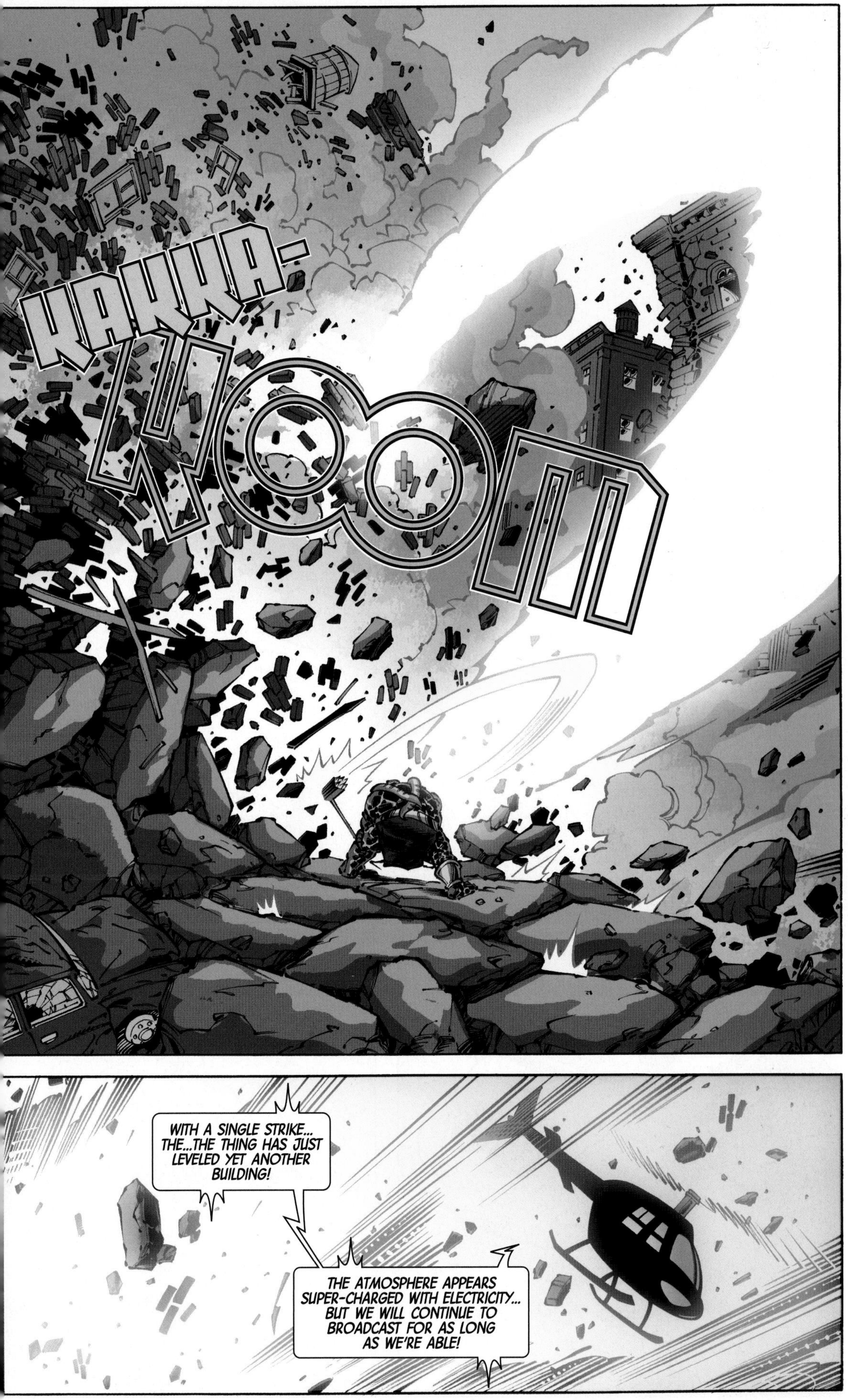
KAKKA-
KOOM
WITH A SINGLE STRIKE... THE...THE THING HAS JUST LEVELED YET ANOTHER BUILDING!
THE ATMOSPHERE APPEARS SUPER-CHARGED WITH ELECTRICITY... BUT WE WILL CONTINUE TO BROADCAST FOR AS LONG AS WE'RE ABLE!

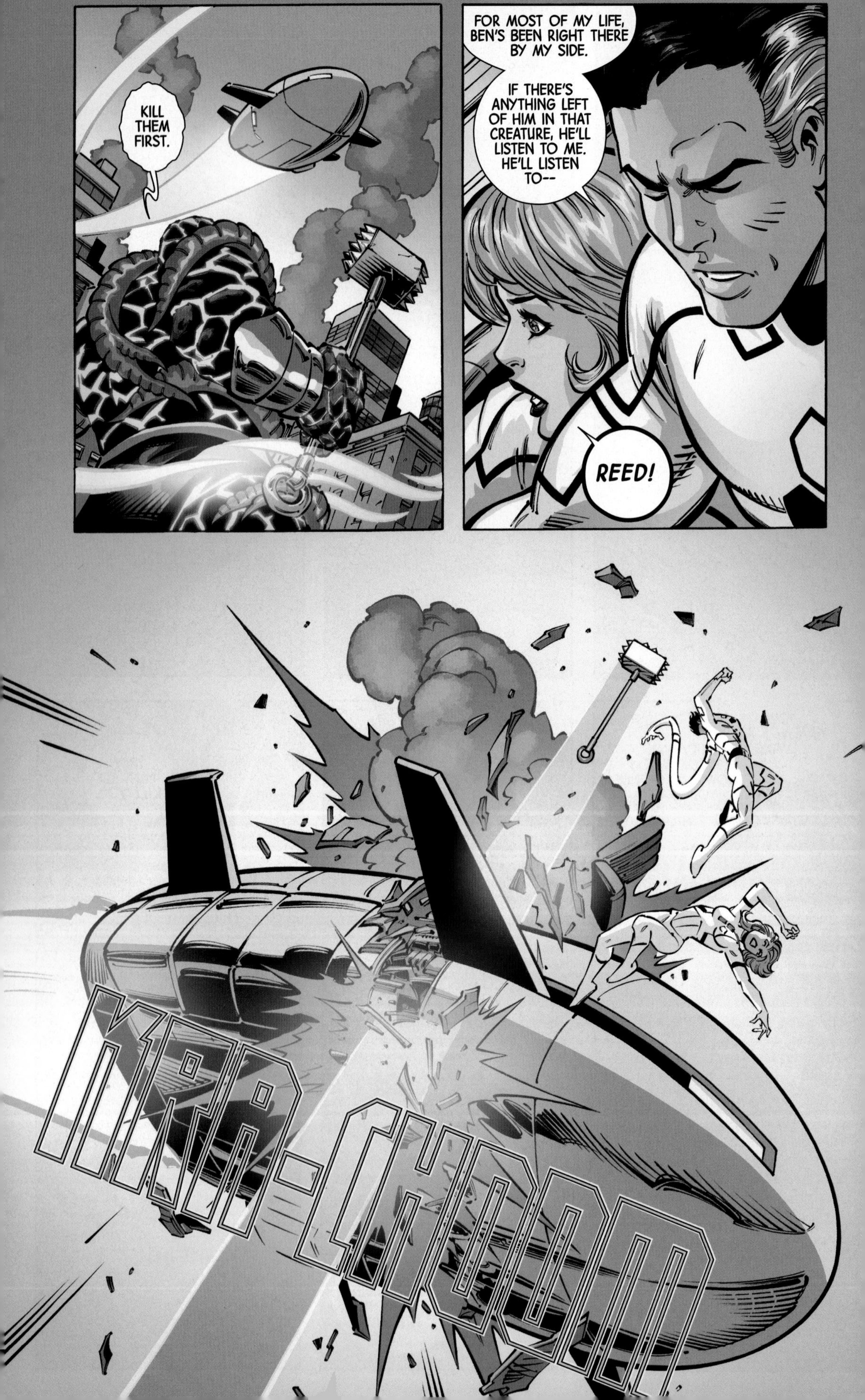
KILL THEM FIRST.
FOR MOST OF MY LIFE, BEN'S BEEN RIGHT THERE BY MY SIDE.
IF THERE'S ANYTHING LEFT OF HIM IN THAT CREATURE, HE'LL LISTEN TO ME. HE'LL LISTEN TO--
REED!
KRA-CHOOM

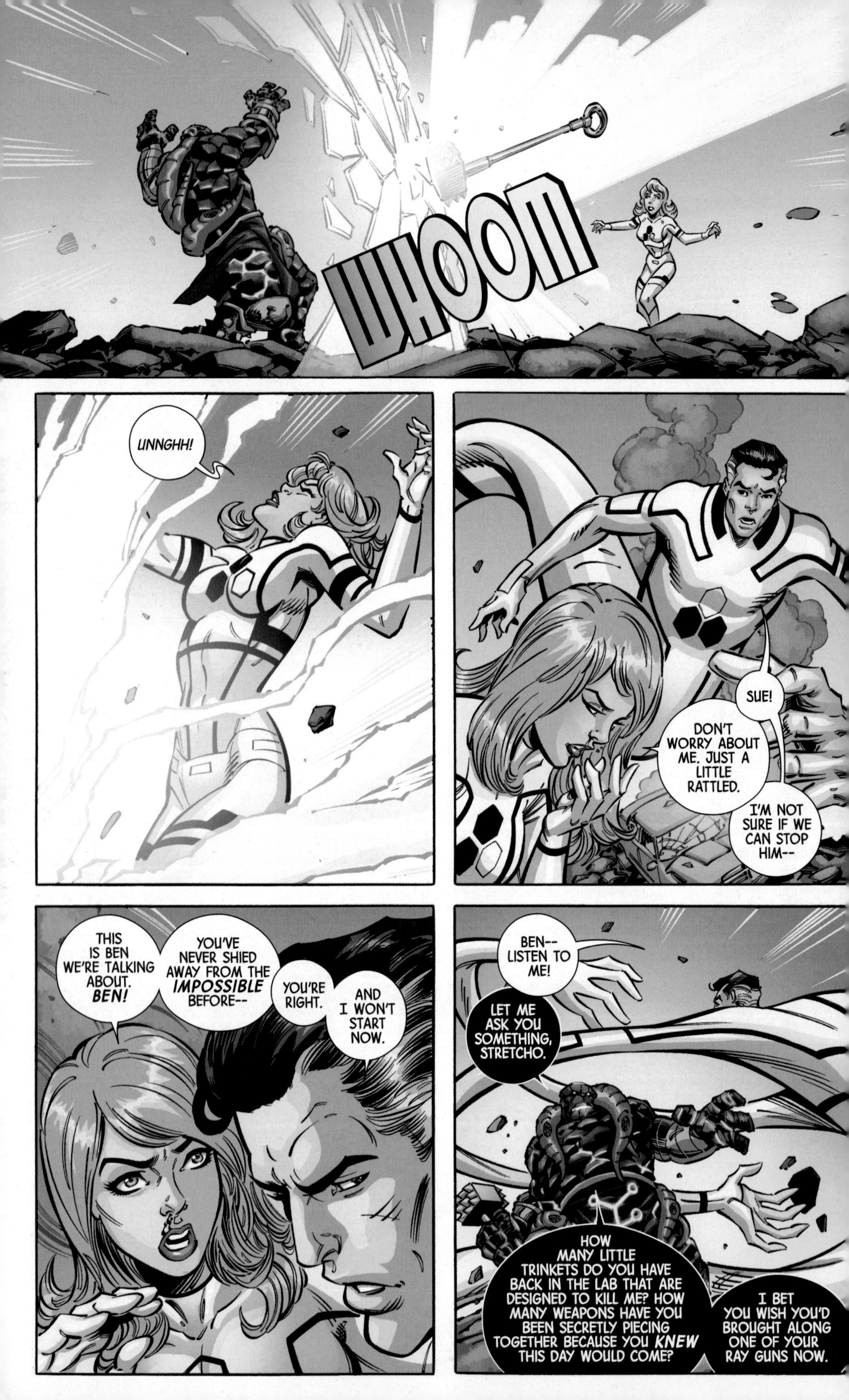
WHOOM
UNNGHH!
SUE!
DON'T WORRY ABOUT ME. JUST A LITTLE RATTLED.
I'M NOT SURE IF WE CAN STOP HIM--
THIS IS BEN WE'RE TALKING ABOUT. *BEN!*
YOU'VE NEVER SHIED AWAY FROM THE *IMPOSSIBLE* BEFORE--
YOU'RE RIGHT.
AND I WON'T START NOW.
BEN-- LISTEN TO ME!
LET ME ASK YOU SOMETHING, STRETCHO.
HOW MANY LITTLE TRINKETS DO YOU HAVE BACK IN THE LAB THAT ARE DESIGNED TO KILL ME? HOW MANY WEAPONS HAVE YOU BEEN SECRETLY PIECING TOGETHER BECAUSE YOU *KNEW* THIS DAY WOULD COME?
I BET YOU WISH YOU'D BROUGHT ALONG ONE OF YOUR RAY GUNS NOW.

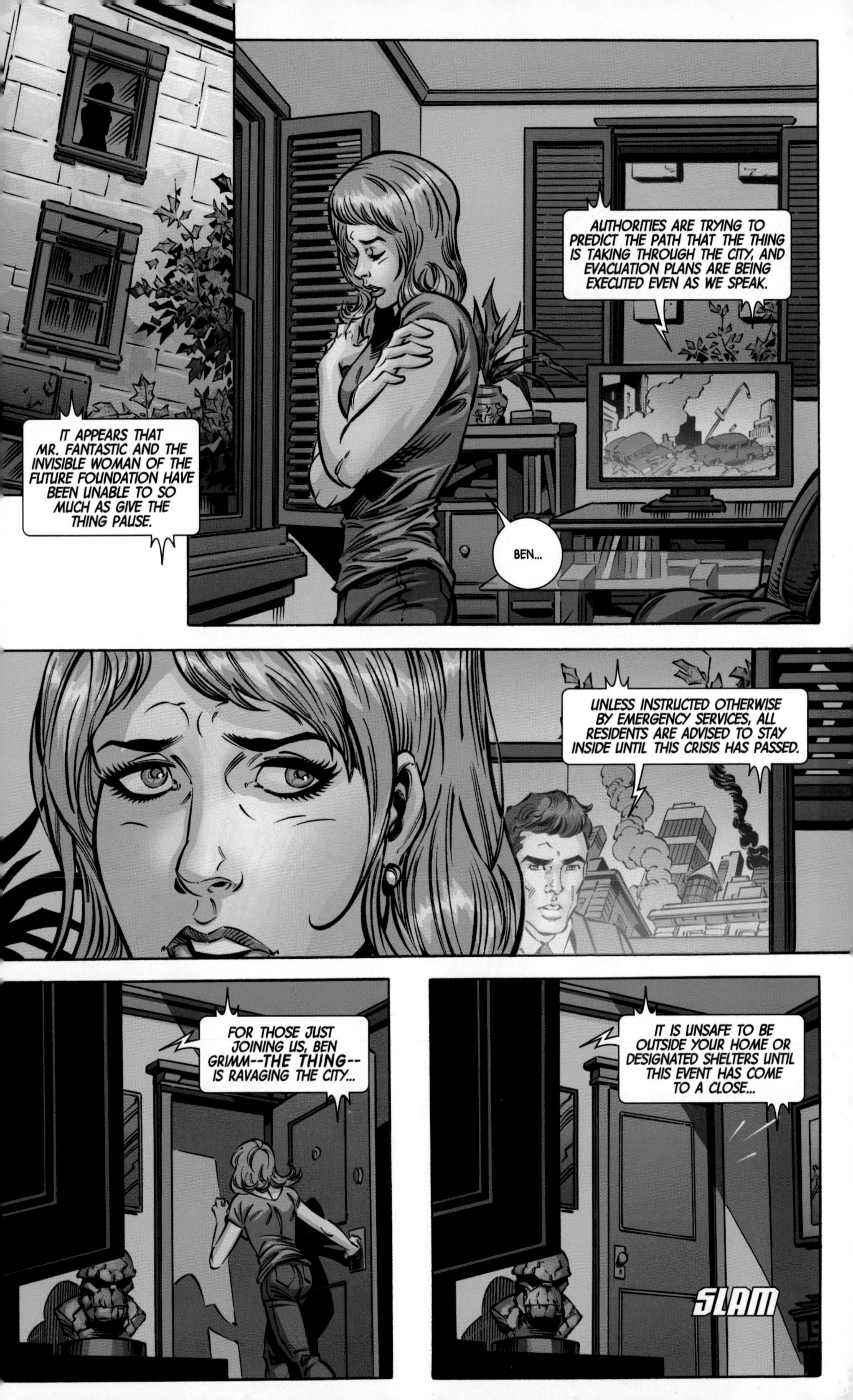
AUTHORITIES ARE TRYING TO PREDICT THE PATH THAT THE THING IS TAKING THROUGH THE CITY, AND EVACUATION PLANS ARE BEING EXECUTED EVEN AS WE SPEAK.
IT APPEARS THAT MR. FANTASTIC AND THE INVISIBLE WOMAN OF THE FUTURE FOUNDATION HAVE BEEN UNABLE TO SO MUCH AS GIVE THE THING PAUSE.
BEN...
UNLESS INSTRUCTED OTHERWISE BY EMERGENCY SERVICES, ALL RESIDENTS ARE ADVISED TO STAY INSIDE UNTIL THIS CRISIS HAS PASSED.
FOR THOSE JUST JOINING US, BEN GRIMM--THE THING--IS RAVAGING THE CITY...
IT IS UNSAFE TO BE OUTSIDE YOUR HOME OR DESIGNATED SHELTERS UNTIL THIS EVENT HAS COME TO A CLOSE...
SLAM

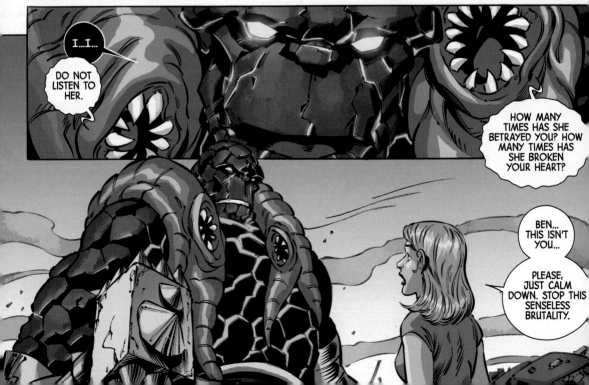

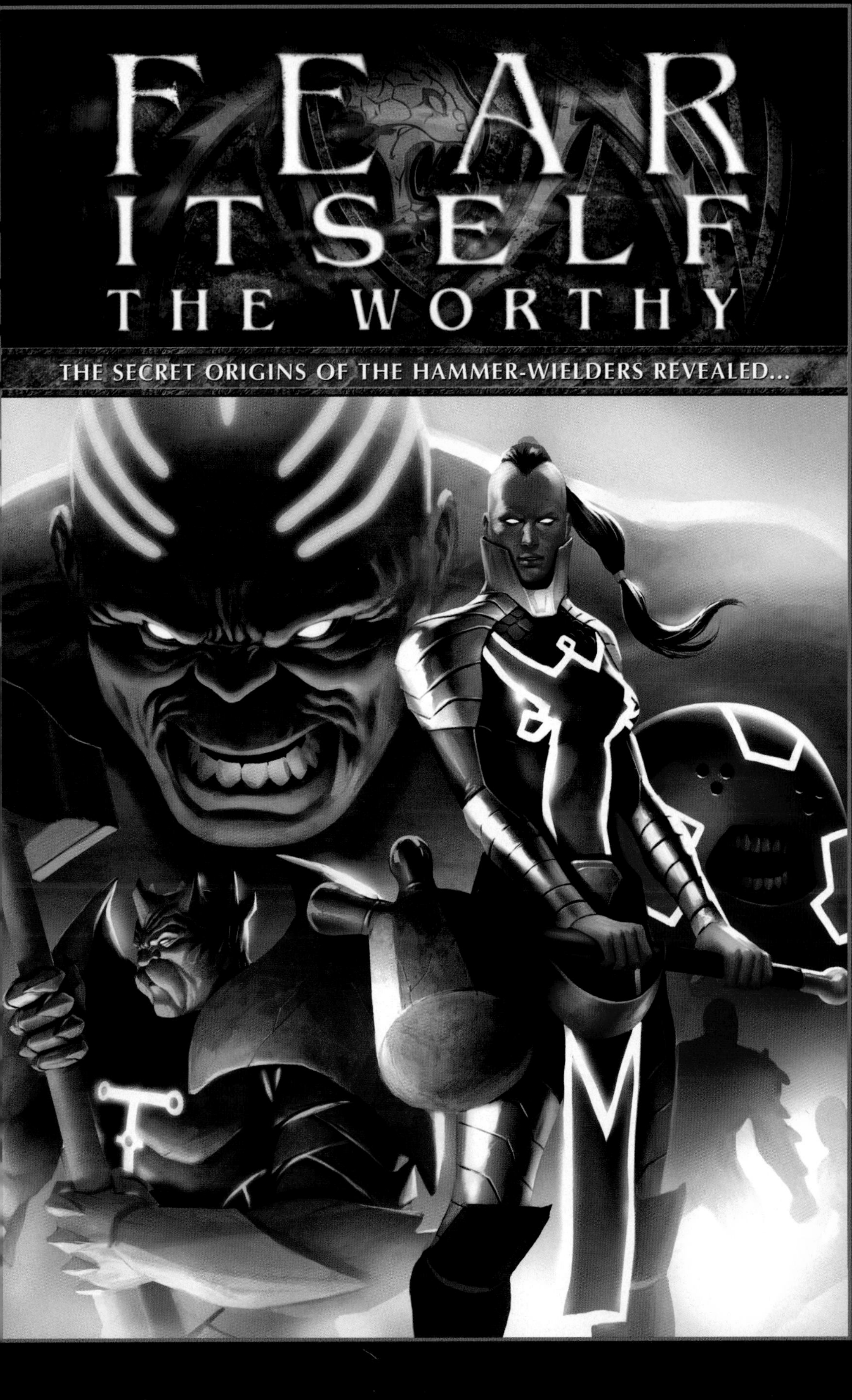
FEAR ITSELF
THE WORTHY
THE SECRET ORIGINS OF THE HAMMER-WIELDERS REVEALED...

THE WORTHY

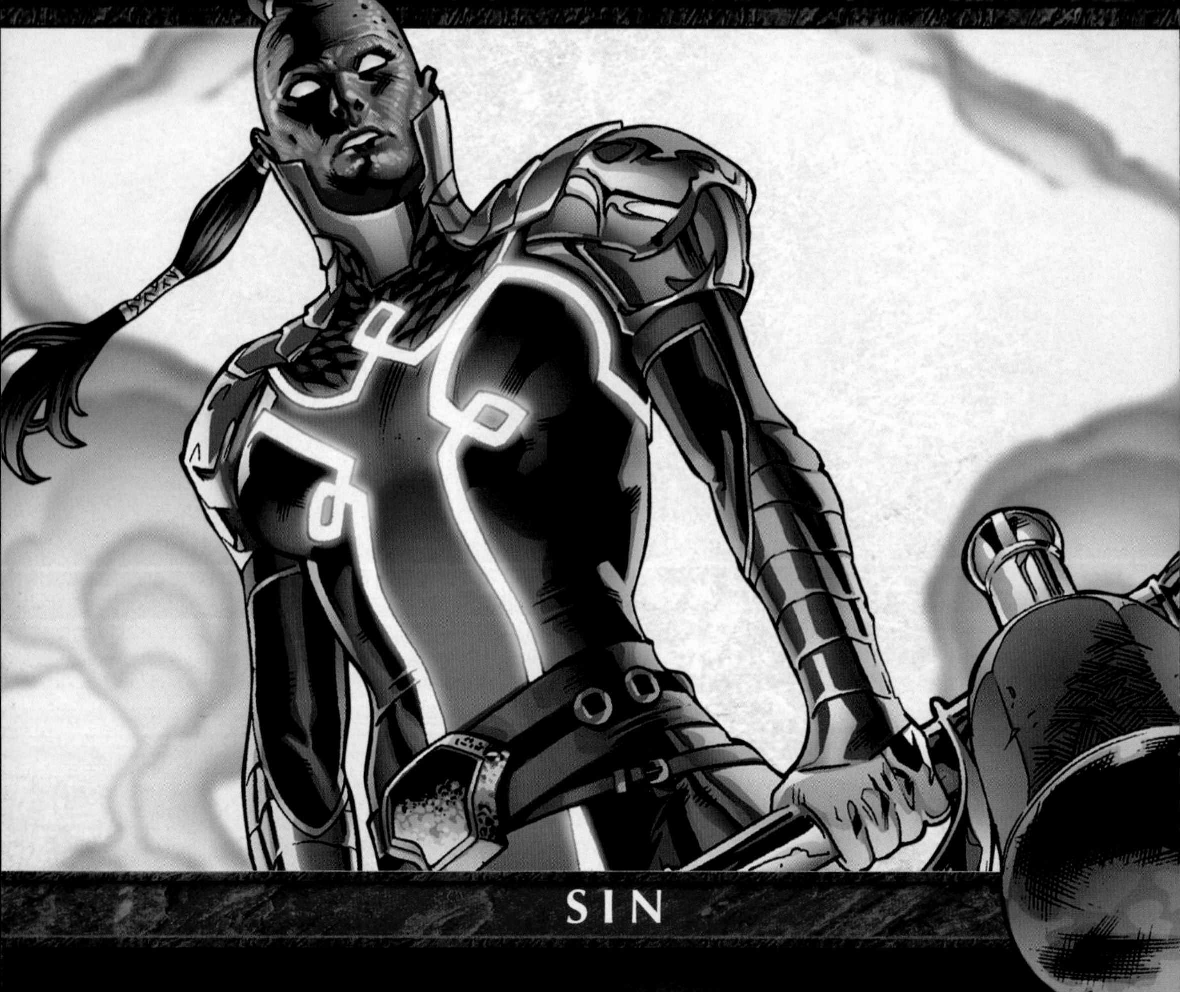

SIN

SKADI

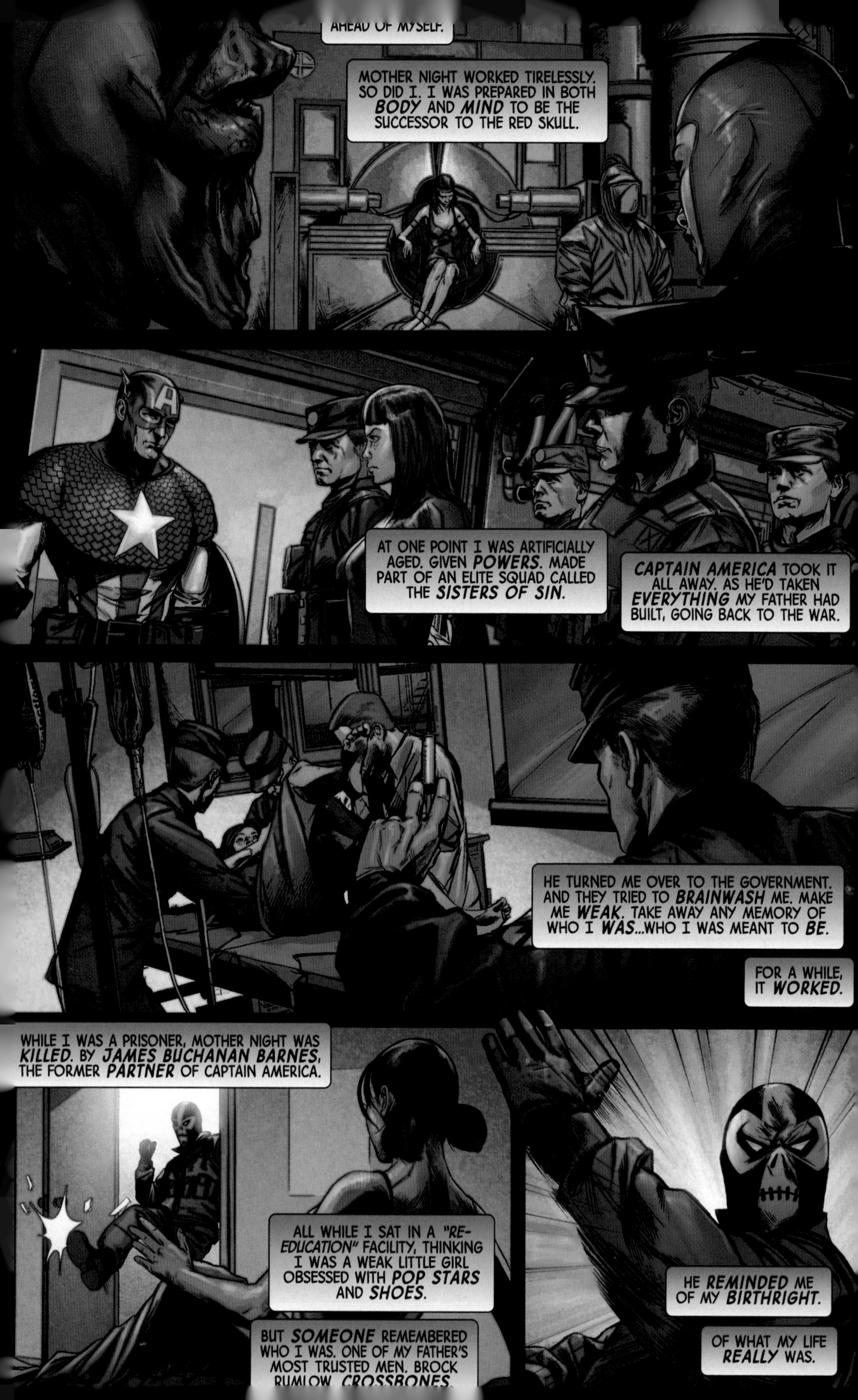
AHEAD OF MYSELF.
MOTHER NIGHT WORKED TIRELESSLY. SO DID I. I WAS PREPARED IN BOTH BODY AND MIND TO BE THE SUCCESSOR TO THE RED SKULL.
AT ONE POINT I WAS ARTIFICIALLY AGED. GIVEN POWERS. MADE PART OF AN ELITE SQUAD CALLED THE SISTERS OF SIN.
CAPTAIN AMERICA TOOK IT ALL AWAY. AS HE'D TAKEN EVERYTHING MY FATHER HAD BUILT, GOING BACK TO THE WAR.
HE TURNED ME OVER TO THE GOVERNMENT. AND THEY TRIED TO BRAINWASH ME. MAKE ME WEAK. TAKE AWAY ANY MEMORY OF WHO I WAS...WHO I WAS MEANT TO BE.
FOR A WHILE, IT WORKED.
WHILE I WAS A PRISONER, MOTHER NIGHT WAS KILLED. BY JAMES BUCHANAN BARNES, THE FORMER PARTNER OF CAPTAIN AMERICA.
ALL WHILE I SAT IN A "RE-EDUCATION" FACILITY, THINKING I WAS A WEAK LITTLE GIRL OBSESSED WITH POP STARS AND SHOES.
BUT SOMEONE REMEMBERED WHO I WAS. ONE OF MY FATHER'S MOST TRUSTED MEN. BROCK RUMLOW. CROSSBONES.
HE REMINDED ME OF MY BIRTHRIGHT.
OF WHAT MY LIFE REALLY WAS.

THE WORTHY

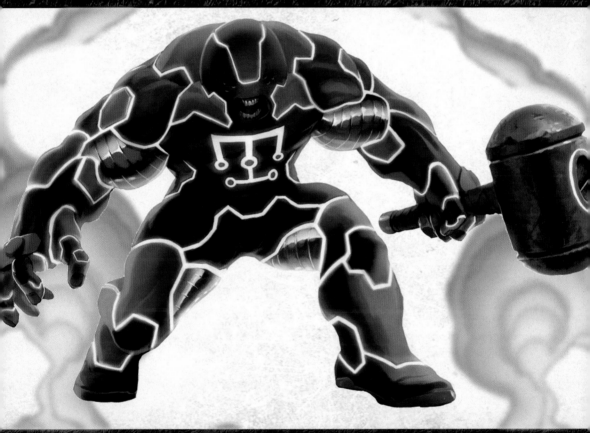

JUGGERNAUT

KUURTH:
BREAKER OF STONE

THE WORTHY

TITANIA

SKIRN:
BREAKER OF MEN

MY NAME IS TITANIA.

FARNUM OBSERVATIONAL FACILITY, UPSTATE NEW YORK

JEN VAN METER
WRITER

CLAYTON HENRY
ARTIST

FRANK MARTIN JR.
COLORIST

VC'S JOE SABINO
LETTERER

ACCORDING TO YOUR *CASE* FILE, YOU WERE BORN *MARY MACPHERRAN*--

YEAH, WELL, *THAT'S* NOT MY NAME *ANYMORE.*

I DON'T WANT TO *DO* THIS. I DON'T LIKE THE WAY YOU'RE *LOOKING* AT ME.

YOU'VE GOT THE WHOLE STORY IN THAT *FILE*, ANYWAY--

I *WANT* TO HEAR IT FROM *YOUR* PERSPECTIVE...

...AND YOU *DID* AGREE TO *PARTICIPATE* IN THIS STUDY AS A *CONDITION* OF YOUR MOST RECENT *PAROLE.*

DIDN'T *AGREE* TO YOU *LOOKING* AT ME LIKE THAT, MS. WOOSTER. *ALL* MY LIFE...

"...PEOPLE'VE BEEN *LOOKING* AT ME LIKE I DON'T EVEN *MATTER*..."

PUNY LITTLE THING. NOT MUCH *FIGHT* IN HER, NEITHER, FAR AS I CAN SEE.

LIFE'LL TOUGHEN HER UP...I S'POSE.

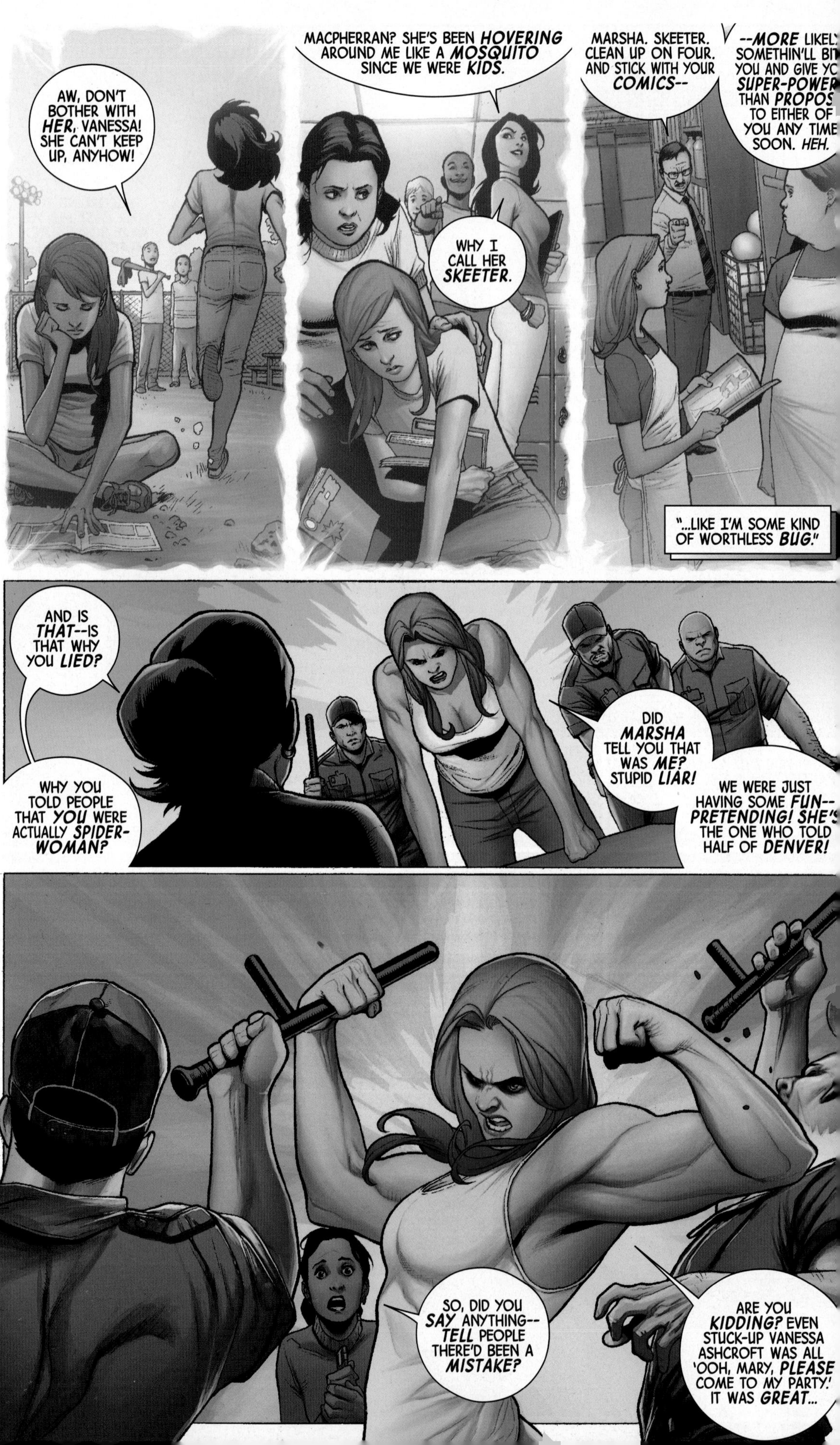
AW, DON'T BOTHER WITH HER, VANESSA! SHE CAN'T KEEP UP, ANYHOW!
MACPHERRAN? SHE'S BEEN HOVERING AROUND ME LIKE A MOSQUITO SINCE WE WERE KIDS.
WHY I CALL HER SKEETER.
MARSHA. SKEETER. CLEAN UP ON FOUR. AND STICK WITH YOUR COMICS--
--MORE LIKEL SOMETHIN'LL BIT YOU AND GIVE YO SUPER-POWER THAN PROPOS TO EITHER OF YOU ANY TIME SOON. HEH.
"...LIKE I'M SOME KIND OF WORTHLESS BUG."
AND IS THAT--IS THAT WHY YOU LIED?
WHY YOU TOLD PEOPLE THAT YOU WERE ACTUALLY SPIDER-WOMAN?
DID MARSHA TELL YOU THAT WAS ME? STUPID LIAR!
WE WERE JUST HAVING SOME FUN--PRETENDING! SHE'S THE ONE WHO TOLD HALF OF DENVER!
SO, DID YOU SAY ANYTHING--TELL PEOPLE THERE'D BEEN A MISTAKE?
ARE YOU KIDDING? EVEN STUCK-UP VANESSA ASHCROFT WAS ALL 'OOH, MARY, PLEASE COME TO MY PARTY.' IT WAS GREAT...

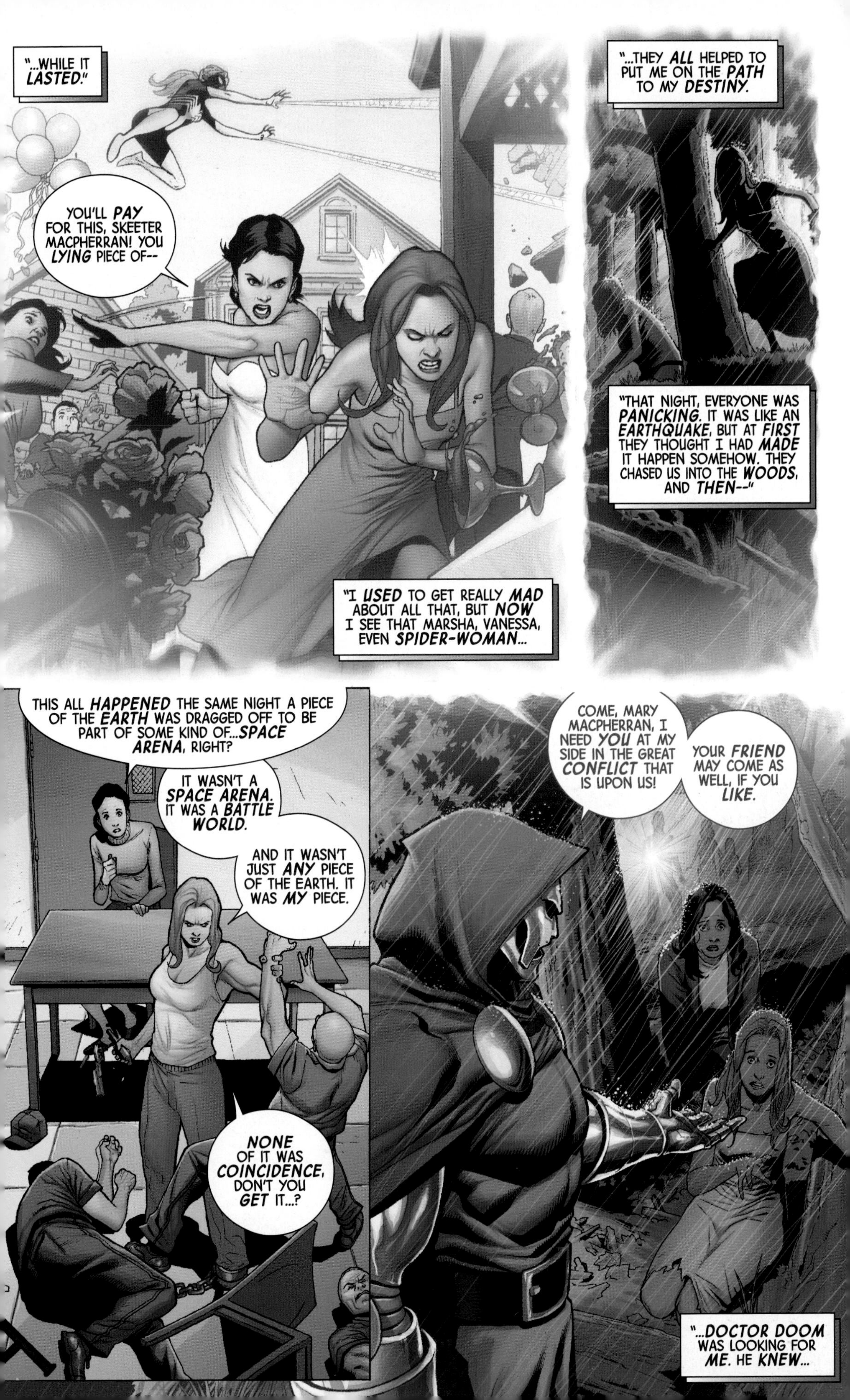
"...WHILE IT LASTED."
YOU'LL PAY FOR THIS, SKEETER MACPHERRAN! YOU LYING PIECE OF--
"I USED TO GET REALLY MAD ABOUT ALL THAT, BUT NOW I SEE THAT MARSHA, VANESSA, EVEN SPIDER-WOMAN...
"...THEY ALL HELPED TO PUT ME ON THE PATH TO MY DESTINY.
"THAT NIGHT, EVERYONE WAS PANICKING. IT WAS LIKE AN EARTHQUAKE, BUT AT FIRST THEY THOUGHT I HAD MADE IT HAPPEN SOMEHOW. THEY CHASED US INTO THE WOODS, AND THEN--"
THIS ALL HAPPENED THE SAME NIGHT A PIECE OF THE EARTH WAS DRAGGED OFF TO BE PART OF SOME KIND OF...SPACE ARENA, RIGHT?
IT WASN'T A SPACE ARENA. IT WAS A BATTLE WORLD.
AND IT WASN'T JUST ANY PIECE OF THE EARTH. IT WAS MY PIECE.
NONE OF IT WAS COINCIDENCE, DON'T YOU GET IT...?
COME, MARY MACPHERRAN, I NEED YOU AT MY SIDE IN THE GREAT CONFLICT THAT IS UPON US!
YOUR FRIEND MAY COME AS WELL, IF YOU LIKE.
"...DOCTOR DOOM WAS LOOKING FOR ME. HE KNEW...

THE END.

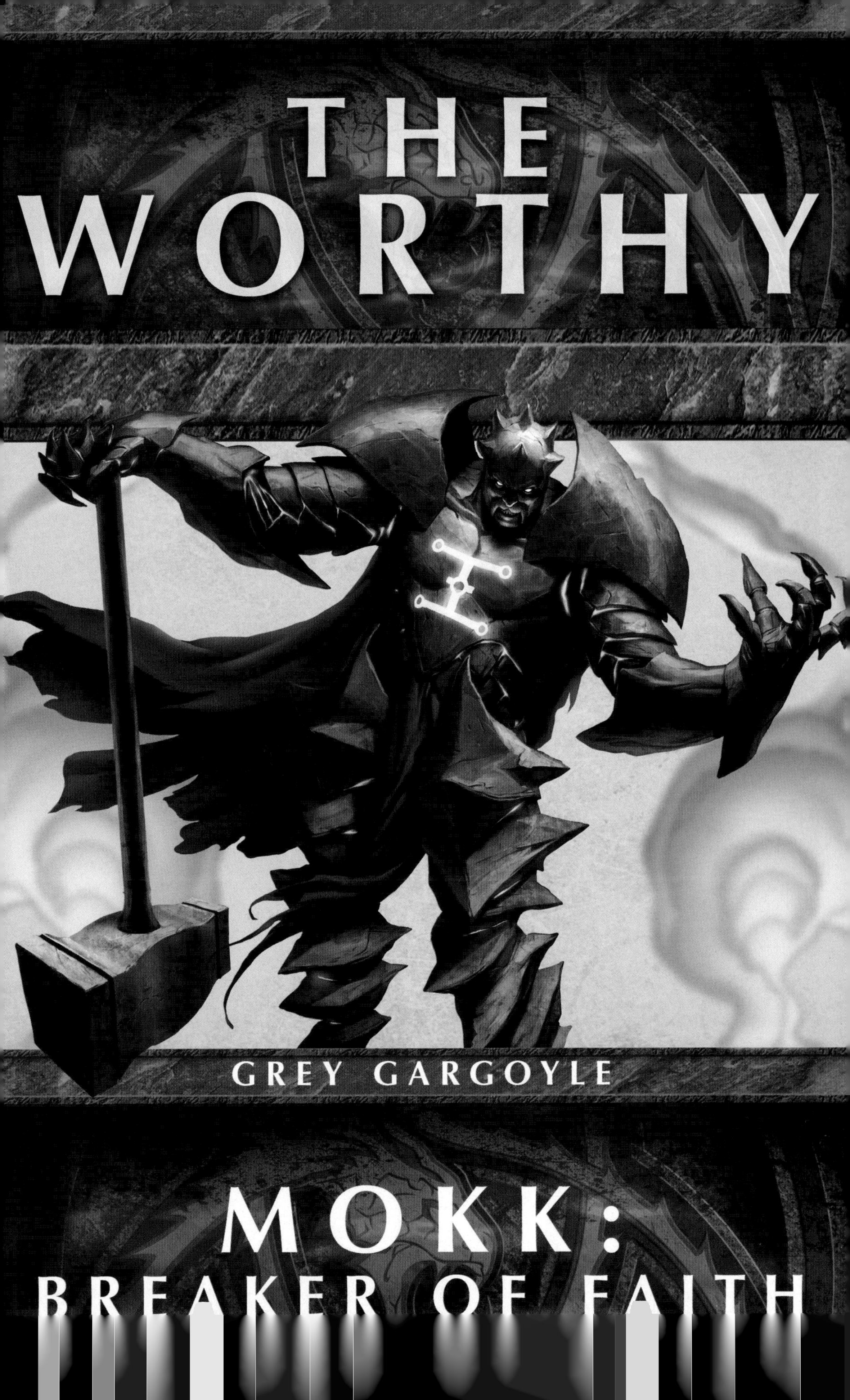
THE WORTHY
GREY GARGOYLE
MOKK:
BREAKER OF FAITH

THERE ARE TIMES I BELIEVE I SHOULD NEVER HAVE LEFT FRANCE.

THAT I SHOULD HAVE BEEN CONTENT TO EXIST HERE, THRIVING IN MY OWN LITTLE CORNER OF THE WORLD...

AS IT WAS DURING THOSE INITIAL DAYS AFTER MY TRANSFORMATION.

HAD I DONE THAT... WHO KNOWS? WHERE WOULD I BE NOW?

RUNNING MY OWN CRIMINAL EMPIRE, PERHAPS? WOULD I BE PARIS' HOOD?

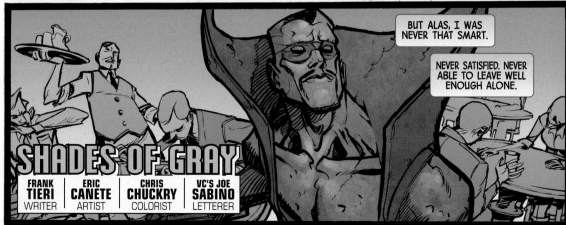

BUT ALAS, I WAS NEVER THAT SMART.

NEVER SATISFIED. NEVER ABLE TO LEAVE WELL ENOUGH ALONE.

SHADES OF GRAY

| FRANK **TIERI** WRITER | ERIC **CANETE** ARTIST | CHRIS **CHUCKRY** COLORIST | VC'S JOE **SABINO** LETTERER |

IT'S BEEN THAT WAY MY ENTIRE LIFE.

EVER WOULD I BE SEDUCED BY THE LURE OF BIGGER AND BETTER.

AND NOTHING WAS BIGGER THAN THOR.

OH, WHAT BATTLE WE HAD IN THAT FIRST ENCOUNTER! HERE I WAS, GOING TOE-TO-TOE WITH AN ACTUAL, REAL-LIFE GOD...

AND COMING AS CLOSE TO DEFEATING HIM AS ANY MORTAL EVER HAS.

IN FACT, IT WAS NOT LONG AFTER THAT WHEN I WOULD TRULY CEMENT MYSELF AS A FORCE TO BE RECKONED WITH...

SUCCEEDING AS I DID IN TURNING THOR'S FELLOW AVENGER, IRON MAN, TO STONE.

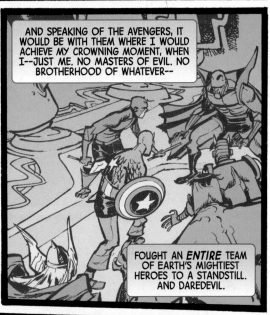

AND SPEAKING OF THE AVENGERS, IT WOULD BE WITH THEM WHERE I WOULD ACHIEVE MY CROWNING MOMENT, WHEN I--JUST ME. NO MASTERS OF EVIL. NO BROTHERHOOD OF WHATEVER--

FOUGHT AN *ENTIRE* TEAM OF EARTH'S MIGHTIEST HEROES TO A STANDSTILL. AND DAREDEVIL.

HMN. THE AVENGERS.

AND DAREDEVIL.

HOW MANY OF MY KIND COULD SAY THAT?

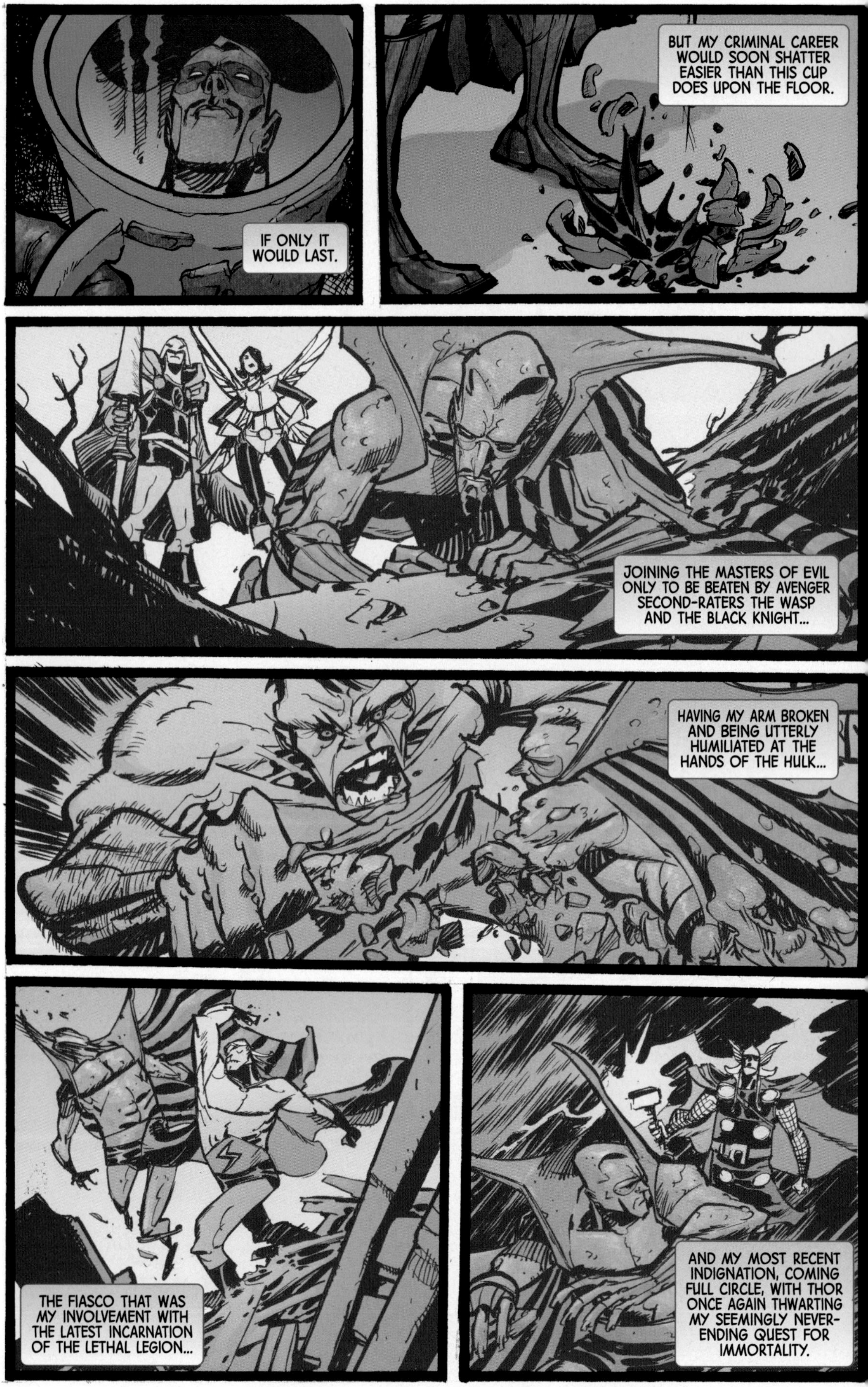
IF ONLY IT WOULD LAST.
BUT MY CRIMINAL CAREER WOULD SOON SHATTER EASIER THAN THIS CUP DOES UPON THE FLOOR.
JOINING THE MASTERS OF EVIL ONLY TO BE BEATEN BY AVENGER SECOND-RATERS THE WASP AND THE BLACK KNIGHT...
HAVING MY ARM BROKEN AND BEING UTTERLY HUMILIATED AT THE HANDS OF THE HULK...
THE FIASCO THAT WAS MY INVOLVEMENT WITH THE LATEST INCARNATION OF THE LETHAL LEGION...
AND MY MOST RECENT INDIGNATION, COMING FULL CIRCLE, WITH THOR ONCE AGAIN THWARTING MY SEEMINGLY NEVER-ENDING QUEST FOR IMMORTALITY.

THE END.

THE WORTHY

HULK

NUL:
BREAKER OF WORLDS

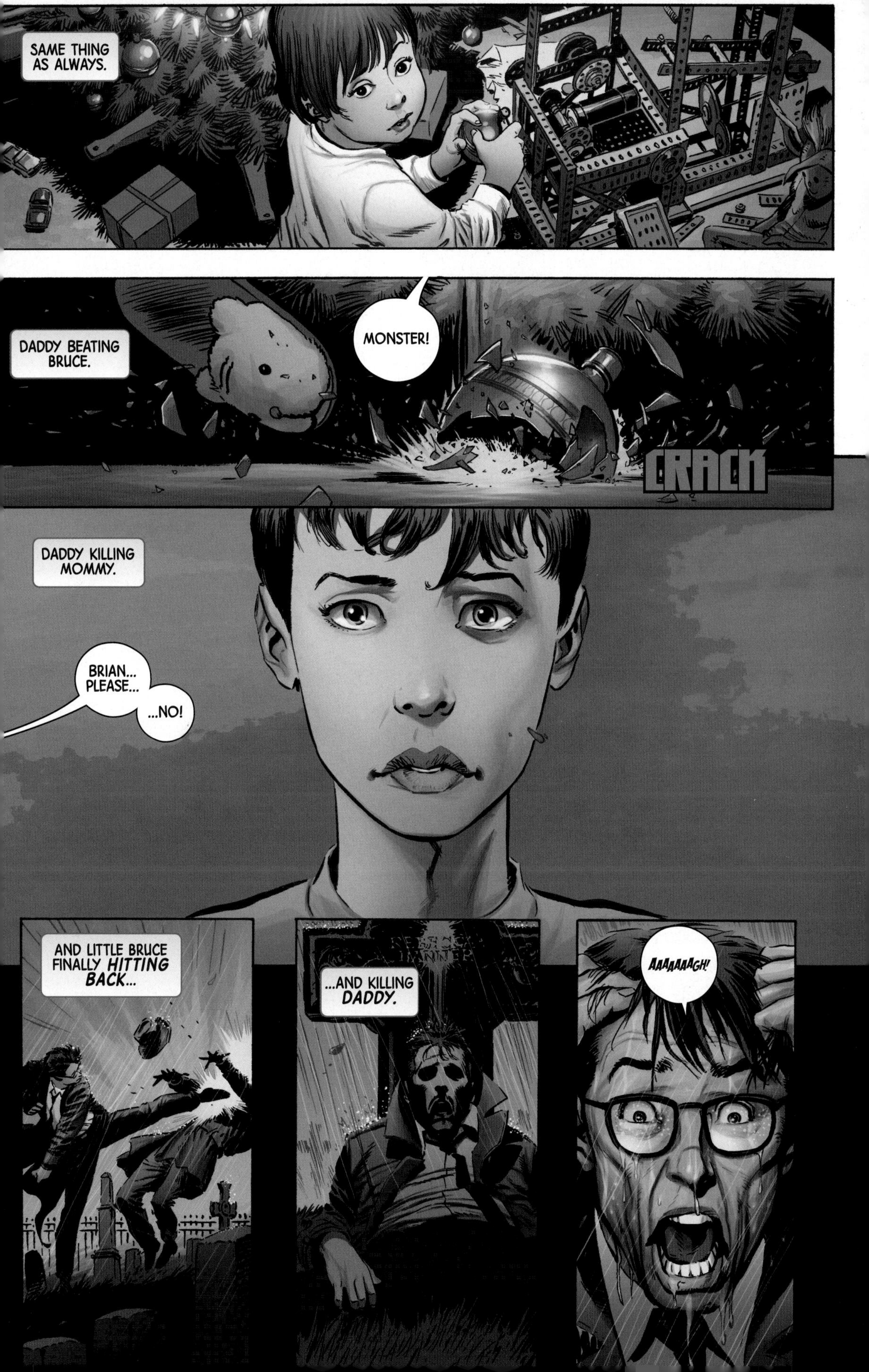
SAME THING AS ALWAYS.
DADDY BEATING BRUCE.
MONSTER!
CRACK
DADDY KILLING MOMMY.
BRIAN... PLEASE...
...NO!
AND LITTLE BRUCE FINALLY HITTING BACK...
...AND KILLING DADDY.
AAAAAAAGH!

THE END.

THE WORTHY

ATTUMA

NERKKOD:
BREAKER OF OCEANS

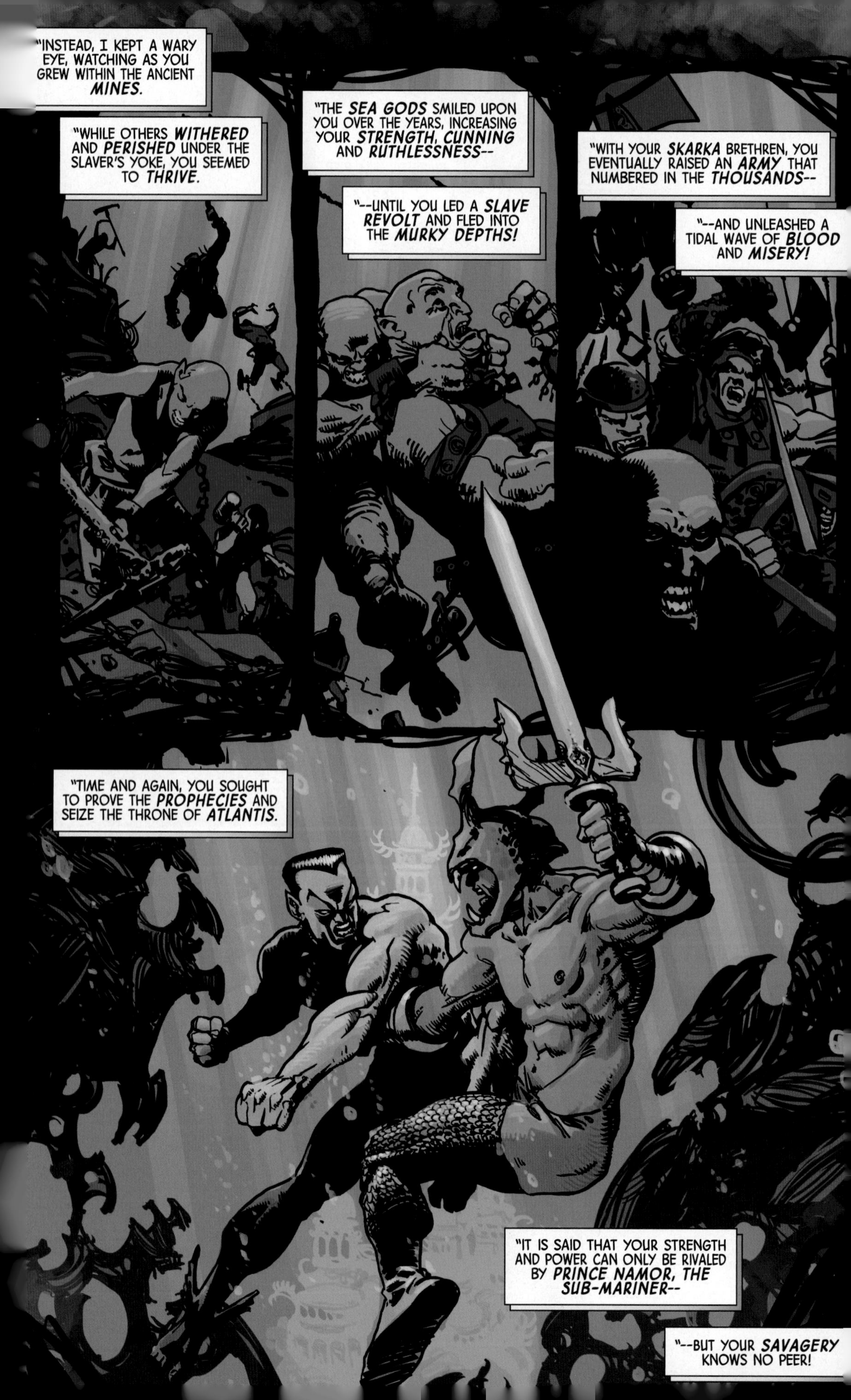
"INSTEAD, I KEPT A WARY EYE, WATCHING AS YOU GREW WITHIN THE ANCIENT MINES.
"WHILE OTHERS WITHERED AND PERISHED UNDER THE SLAVER'S YOKE, YOU SEEMED TO THRIVE.
"THE SEA GODS SMILED UPON YOU OVER THE YEARS, INCREASING YOUR STRENGTH, CUNNING AND RUTHLESSNESS--
"--UNTIL YOU LED A SLAVE REVOLT AND FLED INTO THE MURKY DEPTHS!
"WITH YOUR SKARKA BRETHREN, YOU EVENTUALLY RAISED AN ARMY THAT NUMBERED IN THE THOUSANDS--
"--AND UNLEASHED A TIDAL WAVE OF BLOOD AND MISERY!
"TIME AND AGAIN, YOU SOUGHT TO PROVE THE PROPHECIES AND SEIZE THE THRONE OF ATLANTIS.
"IT IS SAID THAT YOUR STRENGTH AND POWER CAN ONLY BE RIVALED BY PRINCE NAMOR, THE SUB-MARINER--
"--BUT YOUR SAVAGERY KNOWS NO PEER!

THE END.

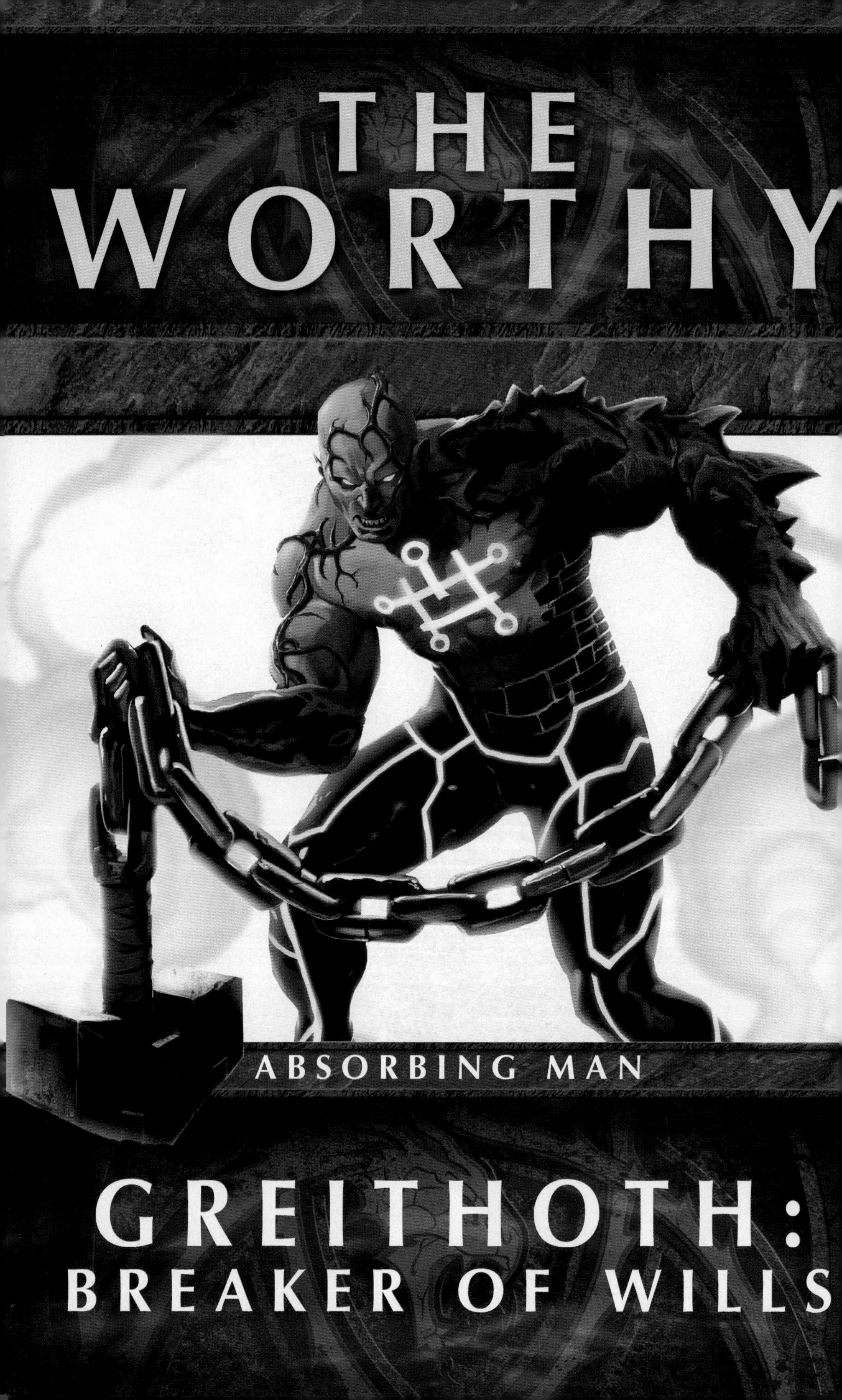
THE WORTHY
ABSORBING MAN
GREITHOTH:
BREAKER OF WILLS

THE END.

THE
WORTHY

THE THING

ANGRIR:
BREAKER OF SOULS

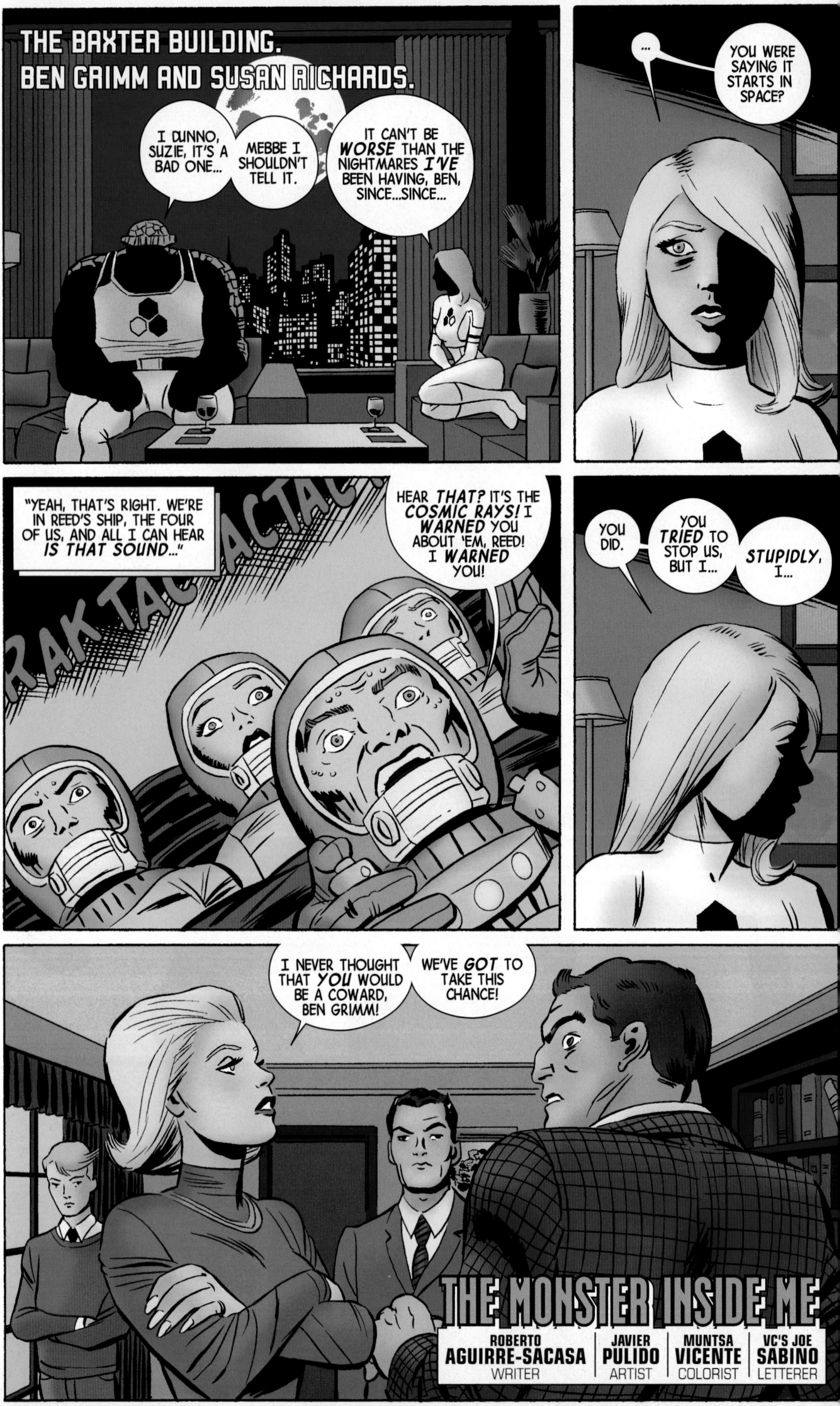
THE BAXTER BUILDING.
BEN GRIMM AND SUSAN RICHARDS.
I DUNNO, SUZIE, IT'S A BAD ONE...
MEBBE I SHOULDN'T TELL IT.
IT CAN'T BE WORSE THAN THE NIGHTMARES I'VE BEEN HAVING, BEN, SINCE...SINCE...
...
YOU WERE SAYING IT STARTS IN SPACE?
"YEAH, THAT'S RIGHT. WE'RE IN REED'S SHIP, THE FOUR OF US, AND ALL I CAN HEAR IS THAT SOUND..."
RAK TAC TACTAC
HEAR THAT? IT'S THE COSMIC RAYS! I WARNED YOU ABOUT 'EM, REED! I WARNED YOU!
YOU DID.
YOU TRIED TO STOP US, BUT I...
STUPIDLY, I...
I NEVER THOUGHT THAT YOU WOULD BE A COWARD, BEN GRIMM!
WE'VE GOT TO TAKE THIS CHANCE!
THE MONSTER INSIDE ME
ROBERTO AGUIRRE-SACASA WRITER
JAVIER PULIDO ARTIST
MUNTSA VICENTE COLORIST
VC'S JOE SABINO LETTERER

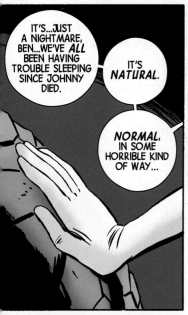

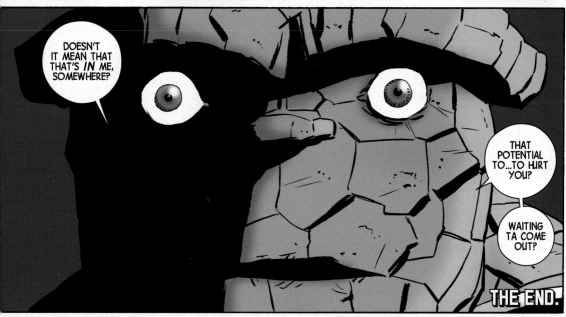

THE END.

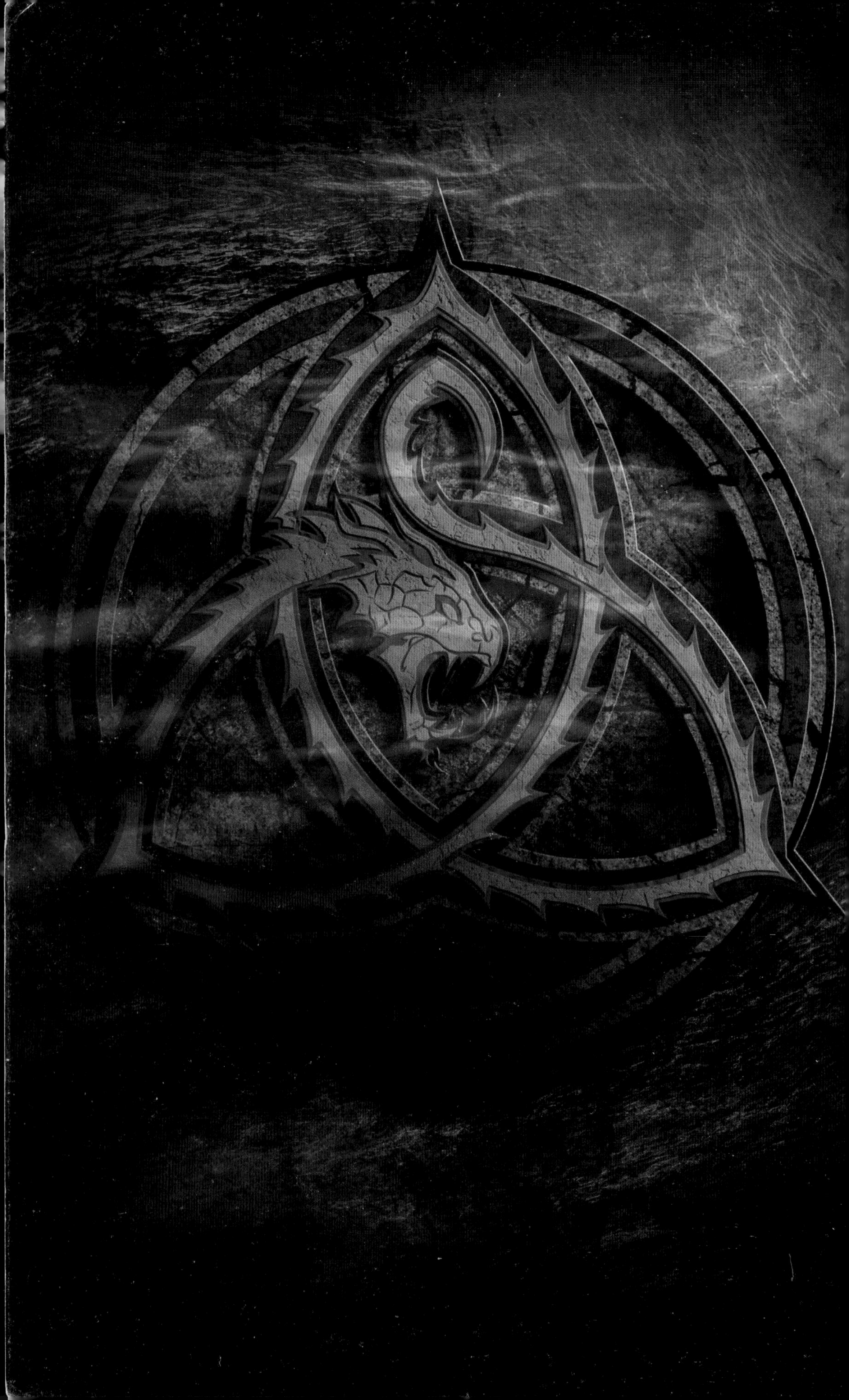